Why Some Politicians Are More Dangerous than Others

James Gilligan, MD

WHY SOME POLITICIANS ARE MORE DANGEROUS THAN OTHERS

polity

First published in 2011 by Polity Press

Polity Press
65 Bridge Street
Cambridge CB2 1UR, UK

Polity Press
350 Main Street
Malden, MA 02148, USA

ISBN-13: 978-0-7456-4981-8

A catalogue record for this book is available from the British Library.

Typeset in 11 on 14 pt Sabon
by Servis Filmsetting Ltd, Stockport, Cheshire
Printed and bound by the MPG Printgroup, UK

The publisher has used its best endeavours to ensure that the URLs for external websites referred to in this book are correct and active at the time of going to press. However, the publisher has no responsibility for the websites and can make no guarantee that a site will remain live or that the content is or will remain appropriate.

Every effort has been made to trace all copyright holders, but if any have been inadvertently overlooked the publisher will be pleased to include any necessary credits in any subsequent reprint or edition.

For further information on Polity, visit our website: www.politybooks.com

Dedicated to
Bernard Lown, MD

Everyone is entitled to his own opinion, but not his own facts.

Daniel Patrick Moynihan

In analyzing history, do not be too profound, for often the causes are quite simple.

Ralph Waldo Emerson, *Journals*

Contents

Acknowledgements

I would like to express my deep gratitude to my long-time research associate, Dr Bandy Lee, for performing the most complicated statistical analyses of the data in this book, in association with her colleague on the Yale University faculty, Rani Desai, of the Department of Statistics and Epidemiology, I also am indebted to Dr Lee and her colleague in the Department of Psychiatry, Dr Bruce Wexler, for valuable editorial suggestions, John Thompson has also made very helpful editorial suggestions, as has my wife, Carol.

Introduction: Murder Mysteries

This book is a murder mystery in that it presents a mystery about murder. Or, to be more exact, a series of mysteries concerning murder, including "self-murder" or suicide. Right at the start, two unanswered questions begin the series of mysteries I will attempt to solve. First, why do rates of homicide and suicide tend to increase and decrease together (which they do) – given that we commonly think of people who commit murder as very different from those who kill themselves (which they usually are – though not always)? The second mystery is: why do these rates of murder and suicide fluctuate so enormously – sometimes more than doubling and at other times dropping to less than half – within the population of the US over a time period too brief to allow for significant changes in the individuals composing the population?

As a psychiatrist, I have worked as a clinician with murderers in prisons and also with both prisoners and private patients who were struggling with suicidal impulses. My question was not "Who done it?" or, in the case of suicide, who was tempted or attempting to do it (that mystery had already been solved), but rather, "Why?" I had also been called upon to deal with epidemics of violence within the Massachusetts prisons, at a time when rates of homicide and suicide had skyrocketed. In doing so, I discovered that epidemics of violence can be brought under control.

Nothing prepared me, however, for the discovery of an epidemic of another sort. As someone interested in the causes and prevention of violence, I had been following suicide and homicide rates as reported from one year to the next in the US and around the world. I noticed that these rates increased sharply at certain times and decreased equally dramatically at other times. Suicide and homicide rates have been reported on a yearly basis in the US since 1900. I was intrigued by the fact that suicide and homicide rates tend to rise and fall together, which suggested the possibility that whatever was causing a rise in the one might be causing a rise in the other. But my eye was also caught by what looked like a pattern of peaks and valleys. Tracking rates of suicide and homicide for over a century, from 1900 through 2007 (the last year for which we have comparable data), I saw three large, sudden, and prolonged increases and decreases in these measures of lethal violence, which reached a peak and were then followed by equally dramatic decreases. Both the increases and the decreases were steep and consistent (that is, they continued without interruption for several years and then the rates fluctuated within an unusually high or low range for several more years or decades), so that a graph of these death rates looks like a profile of mountain peaks or mountain ranges interspersed with valleys. Indeed, the difference between the mountains and the valleys was sufficiently great – with the peaks themselves at times more than twice as high as the valleys – for it to become clear to me that I was seeing a map showing epidemics of lethal violence, interspersed with periods of return to more "normal" or endemic rates.

I had puzzled over these epidemics for years without a clue as to what was causing them. And then one day I noticed that all three of the epidemics of lethal violence corresponded with the presidential election cycle. Specifically, rates of suicide and homicide began rising to epidemic levels only after a Republican was elected president, and remained within that range throughout the time Republicans occupied the White House. The increase began during their first year or years in office, and peaked in their last year or years. They did not reverse direction and fall below epidemic levels until after Democrats took office, with the fall occurring within the first year or two of the new Democratic administration, and the rates usually reaching their lowest point during the last year or years in which a Democratic president occupied the White House. When I subjected these yearly changes to a statistical analysis, I found that in all three cases – for suicide, for homicide, and for total lethal violence (meaning suicide and homicide rates combined) – the association between political party and lethal violence rates was statistically significant. Suicide and homicide increased when Republicans were in the White House and decreased under Democratic administrations, with a magnitude and consistency that could not be attributed to chance alone.

My first thought was: how can this be? Surely, it can't be that simple. And of course it is not that simple. It cannot be simply the political label of the party of the president that raises or lowers violent death rates. If there is a causal relationship between party and violent death, rather than a chance correlation, then it would seem almost self-evident that it must lie in the differences between the policies and achievements of the two parties, and the effect that those differences have on people's behavior. But are there such differences, and can they be demonstrated to have that effect on violent death rates?

And why do suicide and homicide rates parallel each other? The statistics, no matter how significant, fly in the face of common assumptions made about violent behavior. People who commit suicide are generally considered to be either sad or mad; they are patients usually seen in a psychiatric office or hospital. People who commit homicide are usually seen as criminals and considered to be bad. They are commonly regarded as needing not treatment but punishment, and they are found, for the most part, in prisons, not mental hospitals or private offices. Similarly, the causes of suicidal and homicidal behavior are commonly viewed as residing within the individual. We expect people who kill themselves to have a history of depression, a genetic predisposition to depression, or some other psychiatric illness, or to have suffered from extreme trauma or physical illness, such as terminal cancer. People who kill others, by contrast, are usually regarded as moral monsters – sociopaths, criminals, "bad seeds," or just plain "evil." Even though the statistics show that suicide and homicide rates parallel each other and that both are associated with the presidential election cycle, and these data are compiled by civil servants, trained epidemiologists, and statisticians employed by the National Center for Health Statistics of the US Public Health Service, it is hard to believe these statistics without reconsidering most of the assumptions we have been accustomed to making about who commits suicide and homicide and why.

So, in fact, the matter is not simple, and the mystery deepens. It is true that a correlation, no matter how unlikely it is to be due to chance, does not prove causation. Remember the tongue-in-cheek claim that the stock market declines after a team from the American Football Conference wins the Super Bowl, and soars when a team from the National Conference wins? Apparently this has been true 33 out of 41 years, a success rate of 80%![1] Sometimes, as in this instance, correlations simply result from meaningless coincidences, with no plausible causal mechanism connecting the two.

Or a correlation may be due to some third factor with which both of the phenomena in question are related. If heart attack rates are correlated with the rate of telephone ownership in a society, that is almost certainly due to the fact that both of those variables – heart attacks and telephone ownership – are associated with the degree of economic development in the society, and that variable is actually causing the increase in heart attacks (by several causal mechanisms, including

---

[1] Downloaded from Snopes.com/business . . . superbowl.asp on 10/8/2010.

greater longevity, which brings a larger proportion of the population into the age range in which heart attacks are more likely; less frequent exercise, because people are more likely to drive to work than to walk; a richer diet with more animal fat and cholesterol; and so on) – whereas no causal mechanism has even been hypothesized that could support the notion that simply buying a telephone, in and of itself, causes you to have a heart attack.

But what about the correlation between political parties and rates of lethal violence? This is the mystery I have set out to solve. As a psychoanalytically oriented psychiatrist, my training and most of my experience as a therapist had led me to seek the sources of psychological suffering or character disorders in the vicissitudes of people's personal lives, not in political events. As a reader of literature, I was familiar with Dr. Johnson's assertion, "How small, of all that human hearts endure, / That part which laws and kings can cause or cure." Yet here was evidence staring me in the face indicating that laws and kings may subject human hearts to the unendurable, or have an equally powerful effect in the opposite direction. To solve the mystery of the correlation between political parties in power and violent deaths, it would be necessary to discover the causal mechanisms by which a change in the party of the president can lead more people to kill themselves or others, or, conversely, can reduce the incidence of lethal violence. How could this be so?

In the first chapter, "A Matter of Life and Death," I present the data – not mine but those compiled by the US government. They show: (1) the rise and fall of rates of homicide and suicide from 1900 through 2007; (2) the three periods during which these rates of lethal violence reached epidemic levels and then declined to non-epidemic ones; (3) the association of these periods of epidemic rates of lethal violence with Republican administrations and of non-epidemic levels with Democratic administrations; and (4) that the year-to-year changes in both suicide and homicide rates showed net cumulative increases during the 59 years in which Republicans were in power (following the baseline year, 1900), and equally large decreases during the 48 years of Democratic administrations. (By "net cumulative" increases or decreases I mean the sum of the year-to-year increases and decreases that occurred during the years the two parties were in power. From 1900 through 2007, there were 107 years in which the violent death rates either increased or decreased from what they had been during the previous year. During 59 of those years, Republicans were in power, and during 48, Democrats. For example, the lethal violence rate in the US was 15.6 per 100,000 people in 1900, and 17 in 1901: an increase of 1.4. In 1902 it decreased to 15.7, a decrease of 1.3, so that during that two-year period, the calendar years 1901 and 1902, there was a net cumulative increase of 0.1 [i.e., 1.4 minus 1.3, or, in other words, 15.7 minus 15.6] during those years of Republican governance. During the entire 107-year period, there was a net cumulative increase of 19.9 violent deaths per 100,000 population during the 59 years Republicans were in power, and an almost exactly equal net decrease of 18.3 during the 48 years of Democratic administrations.)

Examining the data, I conclude that, however I slice and dice them – for example, confining the study to the period before the Great Depression, or before World War II, or after World War II, in order to rule out the possibility that some great but unique historical event, rather than the party in power at the time, could have skewed the data – one finding remains constant: rates of lethal violence (suicide and homicide) rose to epidemic levels *only* during Republican administrations, and decreased below those levels *only* under Democrats. As a consequence of that, the sum of year-to-year changes showed a net *increase* in both suicide and homicide under Republicans, and a net *decrease* under Democrats, even during these shorter time periods. Given the stability of that correlation between the political parties and the violent death rates, and my inability to disconfirm it, the question that remains is: what does it mean? Why is it occurring, and doing so repeatedly? As a physician, my interest has always been in matters of life and death, not politics, and this foray into politics because of a chance discovery that implicated political actors only happened because of my attempt to learn what was causing these deaths and how we could save lives.

In chapter 2, "What Kind of a Man Are You?" I ask: are there other changes in the social environment, besides the change in the political party of the president, that also correlate with changes in violent death rates – for example, changes in the rate and duration of unemployment; in the frequency, depth, and duration of recessions and depressions; or changes in the degree of social and economic inequality? Could changes in these economic measures be among the causal mechanisms that increase or decrease people's motivation to kill themselves or others?

In chapter 3, "Nothing Succeeds Like Failure," I extend my investigation to ask whether the economic conditions identified in chapter 2 increase or decrease depending upon which party is in power. In doing so, I come upon a paradox that constitutes a new mystery: why is the party that proclaims itself to be the party of prosperity and economic growth, and of public safety and "law and order," the party that mounted the "wars" on crime and drugs, associated with higher rates of lethal violence and of poverty, unemployment, and recession? And if one party is consistently inflicting a greater degree of economic stress and distress upon the American public and achieving a lower level of prosperity and economic security than the other party is, and in that sense achieving economic failure rather than success, how could it continue to win elections and remain a viable party?

In chapter 4, "The Shame of It All," I come to the heart of the mystery: the emotion that motivates aggressive impulses to kill others, and the emotional forces that motivate redirecting that aggression onto the self, as in suicide. In *Violence: Reflections on a National Epidemic,* I identified shame as the proximal cause of violence, the necessary – although not sufficient – motive for violent behavior.[2]

---

[2] James Gilligan, *Violence: Reflections on a National Epidemic*, New York: Vintage Books, 1997. Originally published as *Violence: Our Deadly Epidemic and Its Causes*, New York: Grosset/Putnam, 1996. See also James Gilligan, "Shame, Guilt and Violence," *Social Research*, 70(4): 1149–80, 2003.

In chapter 5, "Who Wants To Be Redundant?," I ask whether unemployment, relative poverty, and the sudden loss of social and economic status have been observed to increase the intensity of the emotion of shame. If they do, this could bridge the gap between political and economic events and individual behavior. Although we know on an anecdotal level that people may kill themselves when they become ruined financially, we still resist thinking of these tragic instances as part of an epidemic of violence. We've all heard of "trickle-down" theories of economics, but what about trickle-down theories of violence, affecting both the sad or mad and the evil or bad alike?

In chapter 6, "Red States, Blue States: Honor vs. Guilt," I shift gears. Instead of examining how one population (that of the US) changes over time, I will investigate how distinct populations (of the Red vs. the Blue States, i.e., those with Republican vs. those with Democratic voting majorities) differ from each other at the same time – in the year 2000, and again in 2004. In doing so, I will examine cultural differences between these two groups of states and also personality differences between Republican and Democratic voters. Then, in the final chapter, "The Mystery Solved: What Is To Be Done?," I will solve the mystery of why violent death rates increase under Republicans and decrease under Democrats, and consider the implications this has for the way we think about politics, economics, and violence.

1

A Matter of Life and Death

For the first 13 years of the twentieth century, from 1900 through 1912, the presidents of the US were Republicans: McKinley, Teddy Roosevelt, and Taft. In 1913, Woodrow Wilson, a Democrat, took office and held it for the following eight years, through 1920. The graph in figure 1.1, illustrating the rate of lethal violence in the US from 1900 to 2007, shows a line beginning in 1900, at which time the violent death rate (the sum of suicide and homicide rates) was 15.6 for every 100,000 people per year. It is important to add at this point that these violent death rates are "age adjusted," meaning that the proportion of people in different age groups is held constant because mortality rates are so influenced by age, with homicide rates being commonest among young adults and suicide rates highest among the elderly. Age adjusting is a means of holding the age distribution within the population constant, so that variations in death rates are not merely an artifact of changes in the proportion of the population that falls within the most vulnerable age groups. This

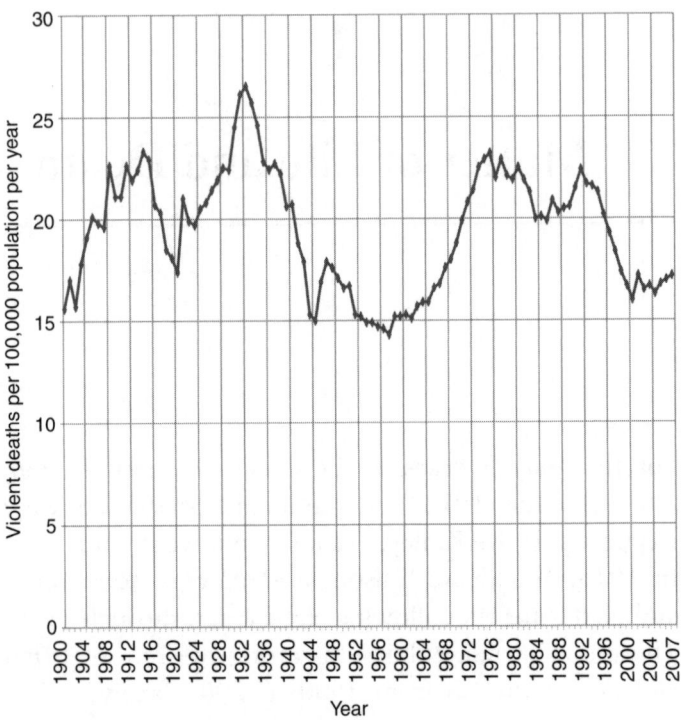

Figure 1.1 Violent Death Rates (Suicide plus Homicide) per
100,000 per Year, United States 1900–2007 Age-Adjusted to
Standard Year 1940 (Not Based on all 48 States until 1933)

Sources: D.L. Eckberg, "Estimates of Early Twentieth-century U.S. Homicide
Rates: An Econometric Forecasting Approach," *Demography*, 32: 1–16,
1995; Paul C. Holinger, *Violent Deaths in the United States*, New York:
Guilford Press, 1987.

is important in vital statistics for the same reason that holding the value of the dollar constant so as to adjust for inflation is important in economic statistics. It means that the changes in the vital statistics that are shown on the graph are not simply artifacts, or side-effects, of the post-World War II "baby boom," for example.

To return to the graph, the line, beginning at 15.6 in 1900, then rises in a steep, upward slope, increasingly steadily, making an especially large jump after the (financial) Panic of 1907, and by 1908 and 1911 reaches peaks of 22.6 violent deaths per 100,000, 50 percent higher than where it began in 1900. Thus we see that during the period 1900–12, when Republicans occupied the White House, lethal violence escalated from non-epidemic to epidemic levels. To make it clear what we are talking about, each one point increase in lethal violence signifies 3,000 additional deaths at today's US population level of approximately 300 million, so an increase from 15.6 to 21.9 between 1900 and 1912 corresponds to what today would be an increase of about 18,900 additional violent deaths – per year.

Following Woodrow Wilson's accession to office in March 1913, the rate continued at its epidemic level for the first year, peaking at 23.3 in 1914, his second year in office, and then began an abrupt, steep, and consistent year-by-year decline throughout the last six years of his presidency (well before, during, and after America's brief participation in World War I), until it bottomed out at a rate of 17.4 by Wilson's last full year in office (1920). In short, the years of Republican presidents were associated with a rise in lethal violence to epidemic levels, and the switch to a Democratic president was associated with a reversal of this trend, ending the epidemic.

But the reversal was short-lived. For the next twelve years, Republican presidents (Harding, Coolidge, and Hoover) occupied the White House, and, as figure 1.1 shows, the violent death rate escalated into the epidemic range again, beginning in the first year of Harding's administration, and remained in a "mountain (epidemic) range" for the entire 12 years the Republicans occupied the White House, with increases almost every year after 1923, their third year in power. That steep upward climb continued until it peaked at the record high of 26.5 violent deaths per 100,000 by 1932, the last full year in which Republicans were in office. It is worth noting that the upward climb began long before the onset of the Great Depression in 1930. The violent death rate had already increased from the low of 17.4, which the Republicans inherited from Wilson's last year in office, to 22.3 by 1929. It continued to rise further, and even more steeply, during the first (and worst) years of the Depression, finally peaking at the record high of 26.5 – a full 9.1 more violent deaths per year for every 100,000 people than during Wilson's last year in office. To give you a sense of the magnitude of that increase, at today's population level, this would amount to an increase of 27,300 additional suicides and homicides per year. Thus the second epidemic of lethal violence also occurred following the election of a Republican to the presidency, and continually increased in magnitude from that time, 1920, through 1932, the last year of Republican hegemony before they were replaced by a Democrat.

In 1933, Franklin Roosevelt began the first of what would become twenty uninterrupted years of Democratic presidents. In 1945, Truman succeeded Roosevelt, remaining in office through 1952. In fact, Democrats controlled the White House for 28 of the 36 years from 1933 through 1968, with Kennedy and Johnson in power during the last 8 of these years. Only one Republican president, Eisenhower, occupied the White House (from 1953 through 1960) during that period. Although Eisenhower was a Republican, he is the only Republican president who did not increase violent death rates significantly after coming to office. Essentially, they remained at the same level as they had been under the Democrats who preceded him.

What is most remarkable about this period from the standpoint of our mystery, is that the 20 years – and even the 36 years – following Roosevelt's election to office ushered in the longest "valley" – the longest uninterrupted period of freedom from epidemic levels of violence in the twentieth century. As you can see from the graph, the violent death rate began an abrupt, steep, and almost uninterrupted decline, beginning in Roosevelt's first year in office (1933), starting from the level of 26.5 violent deaths per 100,000 population that he inherited from his Republican predecessors and by 1941, the last year before America entered World War II, dropping below the epidemic floor of 19 to a rate of 18.8. From 1941 through 1969, the violent death rate did not once climb back into the epidemic range of 19–20 or more. Indeed, for a full quarter of a century, from 1942 through 1967, it did not reach as high as 18 again.

To clarify how I am using the term "epidemic," I calculated both the mean and the median of the violent death rates throughout the past century, which were 19.4 and 20 respectively, and I use the term "epidemic" to refer to death rates that are unusually high, or in other words above the average (mean or median) level. Thus when I speak of epidemics I will mean those violent death rates that fall within the range of 19.4 or 20 to 26.5, the latter being the highest level reached over the past century. Non-epidemic rates, conversely, will mean those that range from 11 to 19.4. (Almost all of these rates have remained well above 20 during the periods I am calling epidemics, and well below 19.4 during the period I am calling "normal," so it makes little difference whether we consider 19.4 or 20 to be the approximate point of transition between the "mountain range" and the "valley.")

To summarize thus far, the three Republican presidents who preceded Roosevelt presided over an epidemic of lethal violence, just as Wilson's three Republican predecessors had. Roosevelt, like Wilson, ended the epidemic; and violent death rates continued to remain below the epidemic range under his Democratic successors.

Let me take a moment to emphasize again that, although the numbers themselves may appear small (an increase in a death rate from, say, 15 to 20 per 100,000 people per year, or even from 18 to 19, may sound like an increase of only 1 death, or 5), at today's US population level of 300 million people, each single digit increase in the death rate signifies 3,000 additional violent deaths per year. When one considers that that is almost exactly the same as the number of people who were killed on 9/11/2001, and that those 3,000 deaths changed history, becoming the rationale for two wars in which the United States is still engaged, these figures are not trivial.

So far, then, we have covered the first two of the three epidemics of lethal violence that occurred between 1900 and 2007. We noted that both began during Republican presidencies and ended during Democratic ones. The first epidemic began in 1905, in the middle of Teddy Roosevelt's presidency – during and following which the death rate increased from 15.6 to 21.9 – and ended when Wilson came to power in 1913, reaching a low of 17.4 by his last year in office. Another twelve years of Republican presidents, beginning in 1921, witnessed steep year-to-year increases in the death rate, which reached a new and record-high epidemic level of 26.5 by 1932 – the highest of the century, in fact. This was then reduced under Roosevelt to 15 by 1944, showed a brief uptick (though still well below epidemic levels) after the end of the war, as usually happens when major wars end (as I will discuss below), and then resumed its decline back to its 1944 level of 15 by 1951 and 1952, Truman's last two years in office. The violent death rate remained below epidemic levels not only throughout Franklin Delano Roosevelt's last two terms in office, but also during the entire administrations of Truman, Eisenhower, Kennedy, and Johnson.

However, once Johnson was replaced by the Republican Nixon in 1969, the rate quickly climbed again into the epidemic stratosphere for the third time in the century. It began increasing from the first year of the

Nixon administration; rose above the epidemic "floor" by his second year in office, 1970, when it reached 19.9; and continued increasing year after year to 23.2 by 1975. It remained in the epidemic range of 21.9–22.9 during the Democrat Carter's four years in office, 1977–80, and continued at epidemic levels of 19.9–22.4 under the Republicans Reagan and Bush Sr., from 1981 through 1992.

When Clinton took office in 1993, having inherited a violent death rate of 21.7 from his Republican predecessor, the first President Bush, the violent death rate began a steep and consistent decline year after year, dropping below epidemic levels (to 18.3) by 1997, the first year of his second four-year term in office, until by his last year in office (2000) it had fallen to 16. Republicans had been in power during 20 of the 24 years between 1969 and 1993. And it was not until a Democrat, President Clinton, became elected for two terms in office that the third and longest lethal violence epidemic of the twentieth century, one that lasted for 28 years (1970–97), finally ended.

The moment a Republican president, George Bush Jr., succeeded Clinton in 2001, the dramatic decline in lethal violence that had occurred under Clinton abruptly ended and reversed itself as the death rate began drifting upward again. By 2007, the last year for which there are comparable data, it had reached 17.2.

To sum up: as the graph in figure 1.1 shows, there were three epidemics of lethal violence in the twentieth century, all of which began under Republicans and all of which ended under Democrats. It took them a while, even with steady, uninterrupted declines year after year, but Democrats ended these epidemics by 1918, 1941, and 1997. The epidemics lasted from 1904 to 1917, 1921 to 1940, and 1970 to 1996, a total of 61 years. And there were three periods during which violence resided in the "valley" range, below epidemic levels, 1918–20, 1941–69, and 1997–2007, all of which began under Democrats (in 1918, 1941, and 1997) and lasted a total of 43 years. The first two of those non-epidemic ranges ended once Republicans returned to power. It is too early at this point to say whether the current non-epidemic violent death range will have ended by the last year of Bush Jr.'s administration in 2008, since we do not yet have comparable data beyond the year 2007. What we do know is that both violent death rates, suicide and homicide, abruptly discontinued the year-by-year decline they had shown under Clinton, and once again began increasing as soon as Bush took office.

Although the violent death rate in America continued falling after the US entered the Second World War[1] in the

---

[1] For a review of the mixed effects of wars on homicide rates (but not suicide), see "Violent Acts and Violent Times," ch. 4 in Dane Archer and Rosemary Gartner, *Violence and Crime in Cross-National Perspective*, New Haven, CT: Yale University Press, 1984, pp. 63–97. They found evidence of prolonged post-war increases in homicide rates in most nations. That is clearly not what occurred in the United States following World War II, however, for these rates increased only twice, in 1945 and 1946, going from 5 in 1944 to 6.4 in 1946, but then immediately began a consistent year-by-year decrease the following year. By 1951 it had reached 4.9, lower even than its lowest level during the war, and remained below 5 from 1953 to 1964. It did not reach epidemic levels again until 1970, shortly after the Republicans returned to power in 1969, and then remained within the epidemic range until Democrats returned to power under Clinton. Suicide rates before, during, and after World War II followed essentially the same pattern as the homicide rates just described – as they did, indeed, during the entire time period being studied here.

closing days of 1941, the decline had begun long before that, descending from 26.5 in 1932, the Republicans' last year in office, to 18.8 by 1941, and had thus fallen below epidemic levels before the US had entered the war. The rate of lethal violence (homicide and suicide), then continued to fall during the war years, reaching a low of 15 by 1944, at the height of the war. But it then remained within roughly that same range or lower, from 14.3 to 15.9, for 14 post-war years (1951–64), during the presidencies of Truman, Eisenhower, Kennedy, and Johnson. Thus the war itself neither ended the epidemic levels of violence that Roosevelt had inherited from his Republican predecessors – they had already ended before the war began – nor led to either a major or a prolonged increase in lethal violence during the post-war years. Although there was a brief uptick in lethal violence rates following the end of the war, in 1945 and 1946, to as high as 16.9 (still well below epidemic levels), they then began falling again the following year, reaching lows of 15.3 and 15.2 by 1951–2, the last years of Truman's presidency, thus returning to the same level as their lowest point during the war. They remained in this same low range during the next 12 years, reaching a record low of 14.3 in 1957.

Except for under Eisenhower, violent death rates during all Republican administrations either rose substantially above those inherited from their predecessors or remained within an inherited epidemic range. While this single exception distinguishes Eisenhower's presidency (1953–60) from those of the 11 other Republican presidents since 1900, it does not contradict the general observation that rates of lethal violence rise to epidemic levels only under Republican presidents. With Ike, they did not rise but remained in roughly the same range as during Truman's last year in office, from slightly below to slightly above 15, and ended only insignificantly (0.1) higher than they had been under Truman.

Death rates from suicide and homicide ranged from 15.1 to 15.9 through Kennedy's three years in office and Johnson's first year. There was then a rise, although not to epidemic levels, during the last three years of the Johnson administration, with the lethal violence rate reaching 18 during Johnson's last year in office (1968) for the first time since 1941. From the point of view of the mysterious association between epidemics of lethal violence and Republicans in the White House, the most relevant point about that increase is that the rate of lethal violence under Johnson, even at its highest, remained below the epidemic levels that followed once this 36-year Democratic-dominated period of relative non-violence ended and was replaced by 27 Republican-dominated years marked by an uninterrupted epidemic of violence (1970 through 1996).

The 1968 election constituted one of the major electoral realignments of the twentieth century, comparable to the 1920 (post-World War I) election that led to 12 years of Republican presidencies which culminated in the Great Depression and the highest lethal violence rates of the century, and to the 1932 election that led to 36 years of what has been called the New Deal Agenda (to which the nominally Republican President Eisenhower subscribed whole-heartedly). The year 1968 was the one in which the Republicans' "Southern strategy" – i.e., the appeal to white racial prejudice and the white backlash against the gains of the civil rights movement – resulted in the radical transformation of the 11 former Confederate southern states and two border states (Kentucky and Oklahoma) from almost uniformly Democratic to almost uniformly Republican in their political affiliations and voting patterns. This in turn brought the Republican party back into control of the White House for 20 of the next 24 years. What followed was the longest epidemic of lethal violence in the history of the past 107 years, lasting for 27 years from 1970 through 1996. The rates of suicide and homicide increased steadily during every year of Nixon's 6-year presidency, crossing the threshold into epidemic levels by his second year in office, when they reached 19.9, and continuing to a high of 23.2 by Ford's first year as president.

Another Democrat, Jimmy Carter, who succeeded Ford in 1977, was the only one of the seven Democratic presidents of the twentieth century under whom an inherited epidemic of lethal violence did not fall below epidemic levels. Instead, the epidemic levels of suicide and homicide he inherited from his Republican predecessors were basically unaffected one way or the other by his presidency, with both rates remaining at epidemic levels during his term in office, just as they had under Nixon and Ford. It is important for our purposes here to stress that the Carter administration did not initiate an epidemic level of lethal violence (no Democrat ever has), but he was alone among Democrats in not reversing the epidemic he inherited. The fact that he was in the White House for only four years does not alone explain the persistence of the epidemic under his administration since all of his Democratic predecessors (like Clinton later in the century) began reversing the epidemics they had inherited from their Republican predecessors early in or at the very start of their first terms in office – with lethal violence rates then declining consistently year by year. During the administrations of the two Republicans who followed Carter, Reagan and Bush Sr., violent death rates, although they fluctuated up and down from 19.9 to 22.4, never dropped below epidemic or mountain range levels during this 12-year period (1981–92).

To recapitulate, when Bill Clinton assumed power in 1993, he inherited a violent death rate of 21.7 from the first President Bush. During Clinton's first year in office, violent death rates began a steep and steady year-by-year decline, finally reaching a level that was below the epidemic floor of 19 by the beginning of his second term in 1997. In other words, it took four years of continuous declines to end the epidemic levels of violence inherited from the Republicans. Following that, the death rates continued to drop, reaching a low of 16 by 2000, his last year in office. The moment Bush Jr. took office in 2001, this dramatic decline abruptly stopped and reversed direction, beginning a slow and fluctuating upward climb. Since we have definitive data only through 2007, we cannot yet assess the full effect of the Bush presidency on rates of lethal violence in the US. At the moment, all we can say is that the violent death rate had risen from 16 to 17.2 by 2007, which translates into an increase of 3,600 violent deaths a year compared with Clinton's last year in office. By comparing Bush's record with that of Clinton, we can observe that, if violent death rates had continued the same decline after 2000 as they had shown under Clinton, the rate of murder, rather than increasing to 6.8 per 100,000 as it did under Bush, would have declined to 2.9 by 2007, and the 2007 suicide rate, instead of increasing to 10.4, would have dropped to 8.9. The point of calculating those numbers is not to say that these changes necessarily would have happened, but simply to indicate how substantial the differences were between the pattern of changes in death rates that actually did occur under each president.

What can be said with certainty of both Eisenhower and Carter is that neither of them represents an exception to our more general finding that rates of lethal violence increase from non-epidemic levels to epidemic ones *only* under Republicans, and recover from epidemics *only* under Democrats. What this suggests is that it is necessary, but not sufficient, to have a Republican president in order for an epidemic of violence to start, and that it is necessary, but not sufficient, to have a Democratic president in order for an epidemic to end.

To summarize, then, the overall differences in violent death rates under Republican and Democratic presidents are statistically significant (that is, they cannot be explained as a function of chance alone). The correlation is strong enough to override both historical vagaries (the Great Depression, World War II) and individual differences (Eisenhower, Carter). Hence, the mystery: why do rates of lethal violence increase to epidemic levels only during Republican administrations, and decline to "normal" or non-epidemic levels only under Democratic presidencies?

Another way of looking at the same data leads to

the observation that rates of both suicide and homicide often fluctuate, sometimes increasing and sometimes decreasing from one year to the next, under both Republicans and Democrats. However, as we already know from having seen the steep increases that lead from valleys to mountain peaks under Republicans, and the steep decreases that lead from mountain peaks to valleys under Democrats, rate increases from one year to the next occur more often, and also tend to be larger when they do occur, under Republicans than under Democrats. And the opposite is true: rate decreases are both more frequent, and larger when they do occur, under Democrats than under Republicans.

When we add together the sum of all the year-to-year increases and decreases that occurred under each party, we find that the Republican presidencies showed a net cumulative increase in suicide rates of 14.5 suicides per 100,000 population per year from 1900 through 2007. And the Democrats showed an almost exactly equal net decrease of 13.3 suicides per 100,000 per year during their years in office from 1913 through 2000. Similarly, the Republican administrations witnessed a net increase of 5.4 in the homicide rate and the Democrats a net decrease of 5. Thus the total net increase in rates of lethal violence under Republicans is 19.9 (the sum of 14.5 and 5.4), and the total net decrease under Democrats, 18.3 (the sum of 13.3 and 5). There is less than 1 chance in 1,000 that any of these correlations between political party in power and rates of suicide, homicide, and total lethal violence (suicide plus homicide) could have happened simply by chance.

The higher the dose, the greater the response: risk factors vs. protective factors

An important concept in medical research is called the "dose-response curve." For example, the more cigarettes people smoke per day, the more likely they are to develop lung cancer: the higher the dose, the greater the response. And the greater the number of years they do so, the more likely they are to get lung cancer: again, the greater the cumulative dose, the larger the response. This provides powerful support for the hypothesis that cigarette smoking is a "risk factor" for lung cancer. Conversely, the more that people exercise regularly (within reasonable limits), the less likely they are to have a heart attack: again, a dose-response curve. The higher the dose of exercise, the greater the protection from heart attacks. So regular exercise is a "protective factor" against heart attacks.

Dose-response curves are one of the "gold standards" in medical research. They do not in and of themselves prove a causal relationship between the postulated causal agent (whose "dose" is being measured) and the response (the effect). But the failure to demonstrate a dose-response curve can under most circumstances be taken as evidence against causality. And when there is other evidence that is consistent with the same causal hypothesis, the existence of such a curve can reinforce the likelihood that one has discovered a variable that can make a difference to people's health.

By analogy, we can ask, could Republican administrations be risk factors for lethal violence, and Democratic administrations protective factors? One way to test that hypothesis would be to ask: is there a higher cumulative increase in rates of lethal violence the more years Republicans are in power? And is there a higher cumulative decrease in these rates the longer Democrats are in power? The answer to both questions is yes. Just as with cigarette smoking and regular exercise, the greater the dose of Republican administrations, the greater the violent response, and the greater the dose of Democratic administrations, the greater the reduction in violence.

In order to simplify this discussion, I will combine both of those responses into a single number, namely, the net difference in violent death rates between the two parties. For example, if the Republicans over the past 100 years presided over a net increase of 15 deaths per 100,000 per year, and the Democrats, a net decrease of 15, then the difference in death rates between the two parties would be 30. All that means is that the Republicans brought about a cumulative increase of 30 more violent deaths per 100,000 per year than the Democrats did, during the time period being studied; or, to say the same thing another way, that the Democratic administrations resulted in 30 fewer such deaths per year than the Republican ones did.

And if there is a dose-response curve at work here, we might expect that, if we studied a smaller number of years, then the net difference between the two parties would be correspondingly smaller: over 50 years, the net difference would be smaller than it was for 100 years; over 25 years, smaller still, etc. And that is exactly what we find when we compare the difference between the two parties' effects on violent death rates.

We can also compare each party with itself alone, and when we do that, we find that the more years the Republicans were in power, the greater the net increase that occurred in violent death rates, and the fewer years, the smaller the increase; and similarly for the decreases that occurred under the Democrats. We find these dose-response curves for both parties for both forms of lethal violence (homicide and suicide) and for the sum of the two (the total lethal violence rate). The consistency of these relationships across different periods of history and different lengths of time, especially given the number of random adventitious events that could conceivably skew the results in one direction or another, increase the likelihood that there may be a powerful and quite specific causal relationship between the political parties in power and the violent death rates, not just a coincidental correlation. That is, given the sheer amount of "noise" or "static" in a study of this magnitude, what is most surprising, and most difficult to explain away, is the fact that the "signal" comes through so loud and clear – and consistently.

For example, there was a net cumulative total of 38.2 more deaths per 100,000 per year under Republicans than under Democrats over the 108 years from 1900 through 2007. Or, to say the same thing another way, the difference between the changes in death rates under the two parties represents 38.2 *fewer* deaths under the Democrats than under the Republicans. At today's population level, that amounts to a difference in death rates representing roughly 114,600 fewer violent deaths per year under Democrats than under Republicans.

If we look at the net difference between the two parties during successively smaller periods of time, we find that during the years 1912 through 2007, 96 years, the net cumulative difference in death rates between the two parties was smaller than from 1900 to 2007, only 31.9. During the 88 years from 1920 through 2007, it was smaller still, only 27.4; and so on: the fewer the number of years, the smaller the net difference between the two parties' death rates.

If one is looking for evidence of a causal relationship that is responsible for a correlation, this is an important point to discover. Nevertheless, it is true that even this does not prove that these correlations show causation. What is true is that the *failure* to find a dose-response curve would make it less likely that there was a causal relationship between the two variables that were correlated with each other.

Another fact that the dose-response curves reveal is how consistent, reliable, durable, and unchanging the correlations between these two parties and the rates of violent death have been throughout the entire 108 years for which we have data, in their respective (and diametrically opposite) directions – with death rates increasing so regularly and continuously under Republicans, and decreasing just as consistently under Democrats, from the beginning of the period right up to the most recent set of comparisons of the two parties with each other (1992–2007) or of one party with itself (2000–7). That does not mean that every Republican administration attained an absolute increase, or every Democratic one an absolute decrease, during its time in office. What it does mean is that even when slight fluctuations occurred under each party, no net decrease under a Republican administration that was already in the "mountain range" of epidemic levels was ever sufficient to bring it below that to the "valley" of non-epidemic rates. And no Democratic administration's random increases were ever sufficient to bring it from a "valley" into a "mountain range." For example, during the Kennedy–Johnson years, 1961–8, lethal violence rates increased from 15.3 per 100,000 to 18 (and in fact were just below 17 during all but the last two of those years); yet, even at their highest, they never came close to breaking through the epidemic "floor" of 19.4–20. Likewise, during the Reagan – Bush Sr. years, these rates decreased slightly, from 22.5 to 21.7, yet never approached the "floor" of 19.4–20.

It is not as though the Republican party experienced an epidemic of violent death during one period and then showed a recovery from an epidemic at another time, or that the Democratic party initiated an epidemic at one time and a recovery from one at another. And it is not that either party showed a positive or negative correlation with death rates only in conjunction with a unique and unrepeated national crisis such as either of the two world wars, the Great Depression, the Cold War, or the civil rights revolution, so that that crisis, rather than the political party that happened by chance to be in power at the time of the crisis, might have been the actual cause of the increase or decrease in the lethal violence rates. For both parties, their characteristic correlations with violent death rates are long-term and repeat themselves from 1900 to the last period for which we have comparable data, 2000–7, with the same pattern continuing through all the historical crises that occurred during this time period.

What may be most significant about the comparison between the violent death rates under Republican administrations and those that occurred during Democratic ones is this: it is not the case that the Republicans have a higher net increase in violent death rates and the Democrats a lower net increase, or that the Democrats have a larger net decrease and the Republicans a smaller one. In other words, it is not that one party is bringing about smaller changes in the death rates and the other higher ones, but all in the same direction. Rather, the *direction* of change under the two parties is *opposite*. The net changes are *only increases* under Republicans and *only decreases* under Democrats.

To make these facts and their implications clearer, let me make an analogy between the long-term effect of these year-to-year changes in death rates, and a different set of year-to-year changes with which most people are likely to be more familiar: the fluctuations of the stock market. Suppose your family had asked the trust departments of two different banks to each invest $10,000 of the family's money, beginning in 1900, and that agreement continued unchanged until you inherited the trust in 2007. So naturally, you then inquired at each bank how much money was in each of the trusts. Suppose that you then discovered that the first bank had been able to increase the initial investment from $10,000 to $35,000 (in constant dollars), but the money invested by the second bank had not done nearly as well; in fact it had declined to zero by 1941. And suppose you also found that the second bank's inferiority in investment results, relative to the first bank, was not simply confined to the period between 1900 and 1941, but had continued from 1941 through 2007, during which time it continued to lose money for its clients. Finally, suppose that you were then going to decide which bank to choose to manage some additional funds that you had to invest. Which bank would you choose?

In this fictional analogy, I have compared changes in something on which people place a positive value (money), not something on which they place a negative value (violence). But if you adjust for that change, you can see that the difference in financial results between the two banks corresponds exactly to the difference in lethal violence results between the two political parties. Just as the second bank brought about both long-term and continuing, recent declines in something of positive value (money), so the Democratic party has brought about both long-term and continuing, recent declines in something of negative value (violence). And just as the first bank brought about corresponding increases in something of value, the Republican party brought about increases in something of negative value. So the decision the readers of this book now face is similar to the one the fictional investor in my analogy has to make: in which political party to invest their votes?

The relevance of this analogy can be brought home by another thought experiment. Suppose the Democrats had occupied the White House continuously from 1900 on, and had achieved the same reductions in violent death rates as they achieved during the 48 years in which they were in power (0.38 per year). Under those conditions, the violent death rate would have reached zero by 1941. Conversely, if the Republicans had been in power continuously from 1900 through 2007 and had achieved exactly the same increase in violent death rates (per 100,000 people per year) as those that occurred during the years they actually were in power (namely, an average increase of 0.34 per year), what would the death rate be by the end of 2007? It would be 52 (a net increase of 36.4, resulting from the yearly increase of 0.34 per year for 107 years, over the rate at which it already was, 15.6, or nearly three and a half times higher than the starting figure).

I am not suggesting that either of these counter-factual thought experiments represents what would necessarily have happened if either the Republicans or the Democrats had been in power continuously. Trees grow but they do not grow to the sky. And yearly rates of violent death rise and fall, but only in very exceptional cases do they fall to zero, or continue escalating indefinitely. Sometimes they do one or the other, of course, as in the complete extermination of a population group by genocide or a smallpox epidemic, or the complete reduction in violent deaths to zero that have occurred from time to time in one culture – or sub-culture – or another. (For example, the Hutterites, the highly religious, classless, pacifist Anabaptist sect that lives in small communal farms in the northern Midwest and southern Canada, whom I will discuss in more detail later in this book, are not known to have suffered a single homicide, or more than one suicide, during at least the first century following their immigration to North America in

1875.)[2] But both of those outcomes, which illustrate the fact that death rates from murder around the world and across the centuries vary from 100 percent to 0 percent, are exceptional. The purpose of the hypothetical scenarios that I just imagined was simply to illustrate how substantial the quantitative differences are between the effects on violent death rates that the two parties have had during the times they have actually been in office.

To put this difference into the language of public health and preventive medicine, the statistics reviewed in this chapter suggest that Republican administrations appear to be functioning as a "risk factor" for violent death and Democratic ones as a "protective factor," in the same sense that cigarette smoking is a risk factor for lung cancer and regular exercise is a protective factor against heart attacks. To continue that analogy further, we can remind ourselves that cigarette smoking is neither necessary nor sufficient to cause lung cancer; some people who have never smoked get lung cancer and some who do smoke never develop lung cancer. That is why even though there is a clear dose-response curve between the frequency of cigarette smoking and the frequency of lung cancer, it is still true that even if cigarette smoking dropped to zero, death rates from lung cancer would not also drop to zero.

[2] Joseph W. Eaton and Robert J. Weil, *Culture and Mental Disorders*, Glencoe, IL: The Free Press, 1955. Bert Kaplan and Thomas F. Plaut, *Personality in a Communal Society: An Analysis of the Mental Health of the Hutterites*, Lawrence, KS: University of Kansas Press, 1956; John A. Hostetler, *Hutterite Society*, Baltimore, MD: Johns Hopkins University Press, 1974; John A. Hostetler and Gertrude Enders Huntington, *The Hutterites in North America*, Fort Worth: Harcourt Brace, 1996; John A. Hostetler, *Hutterite Life*, Scottdale, PA: Herald Press, 1983.

By the same token, we can say that in order to begin or end an epidemic of lethal violence in the United States, it is necessary but not sufficient to have a Republican or a Democratic president, respectively. Just as the tubercle bacillus is necessary but not sufficient for the causation of tuberculosis, the data we have on violence suggest that you can never start an epidemic without a Republican, and you never end one without a Democrat. Among the 18 twentieth-century presidents, there was one Republican president who did not begin or continue an epidemic of lethal violence (Eisenhower), and one Democratic president who did not decrease violent death rates below the epidemic range he inherited from his Republican predecessors (Carter). Since we do not yet have the violence rates for 2008, all we can say about George W. Bush is that, although violent death rates increased during his presidency (in contrast to Eisenhower's), they had not reached epidemic levels as of 2007. He may turn out to be further proof that being Republican, although necessary, is not sufficient.

Why have these correlations not been noticed until now?

Before proceeding further with my investigation, I want to ask my readers: do you find yourself as puzzled as I am by one further mystery about all these murders and suicides – namely, why have these remarkable correlations between political party in power and violent death rates not been noticed up until now? One possible contributor to the overlooking of these correlations by almost everyone[3] who has studied them before may be that, despite the fact that suicide and homicide rates have cumulatively risen during Republican administrations and declined under Democratic ones, the *average* rates of suicide and homicide over the years each party was in power are almost *identical*. The reason for this is easy to understand. To simplify the math, suppose that in one ten-year period, the violence rate is going up 1 point per year, from 1 to 10, and in another ten-year period it is going down by 1 point per year, from 10 to 1. If you add up all the numbers and divide them by 10, you find that the average of the two different series is exactly the same, even though the net effect of the two series is exactly opposite. That is precisely what has happened, time after time, over the past century, with the rates cumulatively going up under Republicans and down under Democrats. So while the Republicans have accumulated massive net rate increases over the years, and the Democrats massive net rate decreases, the average rate in all the years taken together is about the same for both parties. The fact that these two pat-

---

[3] There are two exceptions to that generalization, though both are cross-sectional studies rather than longitudinal ones, and both were published in the mass media (a newspaper and a popular magazine), not a scientific journal. Michael Miller, a psychiatrist who is the editor of the *Harvard Mental Health Letter*, observed in an op-ed. piece in the *Boston Globe* that suicide was more frequent in the "Red States" that voted for Bush Jr. in 2000 than in the Democratically oriented "Blue States" ("A Suicide Map of the U.S.," August 22, 2004). And in a similar vein, *James Wolcott* reviewed a good deal of evidence that suicide as well as violent crime and many other symptoms of social pathology have been more common in the Red States than in the Blue in recent years ("Red State Babylon," *Vanity Fair*, Nov. 2006, p. 162).

terns of changes in death rates have an exactly opposite effect on the welfare of the American people may have been overlooked because of that.

The death rates I have summarized here have been part of the public record, and freely available to anyone who wanted to review them, since 1900. In that sense, they have been, so to speak, hiding in plain sight. An additional reason for our collective failure to notice these egregious facts may be directly related to what I just said: because the increases in lethal violence rates that occur under Republicans have regularly been compensated for by the almost exactly equal decreases that have occurred under Democrats, there has been, over time, essentially no net change in violent death rates for the country as a whole. For example, the homicide rate in 2000 (6.4 deaths per 100,000 population per year) was exactly what it had been in 1900, and the suicide rate in 2000 (9.6 per 100,000) was almost exactly what it had been in 1900 (9.2). That is true despite the fact, as we have already seen, that there were huge "swings" in both death rates when the presidency changed from one party to the other.

This absence of any net long-term increase or decrease in those rates could easily mislead people into thinking that there were no significant differences between the two parties with respect to the rate of violent deaths during their respective terms in office. That in turn would make it easy to forget that the only times the Republicans' violent death rates were *not* in an epidemic range were when they had inherited low rates from their Democratic predecessors. And the only times the Democrats' death rates were *in* an epidemic range were when they had inherited those high rates from Republicans.

In fact, there is only one reason that our homicide and suicide rates today are not at disastrously high epidemic levels, and that is because the Democrats have regularly undone the Republican rate increases with decreases of equal magnitude. Specifically, the Republicans increased the suicide and homicide rates by net cumulative totals of 14.5 and 5.4 per 100,000 respectively between 1900 and 2007, while the Democrats reduced those totals by almost exactly equal amounts (13.3 and 5.0, respectively). If the lethal violence rates in 2007 were determined only by the Republicans' influence on them during their 59 years in office, the suicide rate would have been 23.7 instead of 10.4 in 2007, and the homicide rate, 11.8 instead of 6.8. That would have resulted in a total violent death rate of 35.5 per 100,000, more than twice as many violent deaths as actually occurred – roughly 106,500, as opposed to the 52,000 that there actually were, if we apply those death rates to the current US population level of 300 million.

In this chapter I have summarized some of the data that create the murder mystery. In the chapters that follow, I will attempt to solve the mystery by seeing if there is any evidence that might explain why rates of suicide and homicide rise to epidemic levels only under Republican presidents, and fall to non-epidemic levels only during Democratic administrations. But statistics are one thing and feelings another, and statistics do not motivate people to commit suicide or homicide.

2

What Kind of a Man Are You?

In 1992, a gaunt, disheveled man in his mid-40s was admitted to the prison mental hospital in Massachusetts. He appeared half-dead: mute, motionless, unresponsive. Like a zombie, I thought. Since he was either unable or unwilling to talk – it was difficult to know which – I could only read the police report that accompanied him. It told me that on the day before, he had shot his wife and children to death with a hand gun. The man – I'll call him Paul Williams – was admitted to the hospital and placed on suicide precautions. I waited for him to tell me where he was mentally and who he was.

The next day, when he began to speak, it was like hearing someone talk to you from deep inside a cave. To speak and organize his thoughts appeared to require so much effort, it was as if he were trying to pick up the largest boulder imaginable and throw it, when he could hardly sustain the weight. He looked drained of all emotion, all feeling, and could only slowly and with great effort try to piece together for me the story of what happened. Over the duration of the next few days, here is what he managed to tell me.

He had been a hard worker all his life, and now, in his 40s, he had had a good job as a foreman at a factory in Boston. He was living with a woman who, like him, was African-American, and, although they had never married, each had a child from a previous partner, and they had a stable relationship. She was a school teacher, made a comfortable living just as he did, and he felt she was a good mother to her child and his.

Two months ago, Paul had been notified that he was going to be laid off at work – not fired, he insisted, "laid off." Not because he didn't do his job well enough. He was a good worker. The company just couldn't afford to pay him. Other men lost their jobs too, but that was their problem. (This was during the recession that occurred during the first President Bush's last two years in office.)

Paul did not know what to do next. He felt ashamed, so ashamed that he couldn't bear to tell his woman, as he called her, what had happened – that he had lost his job. Instead, he would get up every morning in a daze, dress for work, and leave the house as if he were going to work. He would stay out until his usual hour of return. At first, he spent this time looking for another job, but then he gave up – there were no jobs, it was too shameful to be rejected when he applied, he just gave up. He had lost his manhood. He couldn't even bring any money home, he explained.

Finally, his wife – as he also called her sometimes – noticed that there was no money coming in, and she confronted him. Cornered, Paul had to admit the unspeakable truth. She was shocked and flew into a rage when she realized what he had been doing for the past two months, pretending to go to work when there was no work, fooling her with his foolishness. And then she uttered the fatal words, "What kind of a man are you, anyway? What kind of a man would do such a thing?"

All this happened with the children looking on.

Paul went into the bedroom and took his gun out of the drawer. He came back. And to show her what kind of a man he was, he shot her to death. Then he shot the children to stop the sound of their screaming, but that did not work. He could still hear them screaming. He thought he would hear that for the rest of his life.

Paul does not know why he did not shoot himself too. When I asked him why he thought he hadn't, he said, "I was already dead. I felt dead. I thought I was dead. I think I'm dead now."

Listening to Paul tell his tale, I could not help but think how often "unemployment" is spoken of as if it were just a statistic, a "rate," a passing number that will eventually change, get larger or smaller, but not affect real people. But as tragic as Paul's story is, what is even more tragic is how far from unique it is. Paul was only one of many men who respond in this or similar ways, with slight variations, to the stress of losing a job or experiencing some equivalent loss of status that destroys their sense of who they are – in fact, their sense that they still exist, that they are real people. This pattern is hardly unique to the United States. A Japanese movie, *Tokyo Sonata*, tells an almost identical story of an unemployed man who spends his days away from home, also pretending he still has a job, until this strategy fails and he kills himself along with his family.

Now, of course, it is true that most people who are laid off from their jobs do not become this desperate and violent. But it is also true that there are always a certain number of people whose sense of self-esteem is so fragile and vulnerable that they are able to maintain only a tenuous degree of self-control even when they do have a steady source of income and the prestige and sense of being recognized by others that comes from holding down a job. Deprive them of this powerful source of support, and all hell can break loose, as it did in Paul's case. Increase the unemployment rate enough, and more such individuals will resort, as they regularly do under such circumstances, to homicide or suicide, or both.

After hearing such a harrowing tale, it may seem a bit absurd to go back into the world of numbers, but it will probably be less surprising to hear that, throughout the past century, when the unemployment rate has gone up or down, so have the rates of suicide and homicide. It was not the loss of a job per se that led Paul to kill his wife and their children. It was the feeling of being emasculated, the shame of being exposed as not a man in the eyes of his wife that led him to get his gun and shoot her as a response to her question: "What kind of a man are you?" And then to kill the children whose screams conveyed what they had witnessed.

In the largest database previously published on this subject in the United States, a study of the period from 1900 to 1970, Paul Holinger[1] found that age-adjusted

---

[1] Holinger, *Violent Deaths in the United States*, p. 186.

US suicide and homicide rates not only correlated with each other (p < .01), they both also correlated with the unemployment rate (p < .01). My own analysis of the much larger database on which this book draws finds the same thing,[2] as have many other studies based on much more limited population samples or time-periods.

In an influential study of the double epidemics of unemployment and violent crime in ghetto neighborhoods, William Julius Wilson[3] speaks of the "direct relationship between joblessness and violent crime." Quoting Delbert Elliott's research, he points out that

> The black–white differential in the proportion of males involved in serious violent crime, although almost even at age 11, increases to 3:2 over the remaining years of adolescence, and reaches a differential of nearly 4:1 during the late twenties. However, when Elliott compared only *employed* black and white males, he found no significant differences in violent behavior patterns among the two groups by age 21.... Accordingly, a major reason for the racial gap in violent behavior ... is joblessness.

It becomes easy, then, to understand why inner-city black youth facing limited prospects for employment would be drawn into drug trafficking and thus become involved in the violent behavior associated with it. The unemployment rate among blacks has always been at least twice as high as among whites, regardless of

[2] The probability values for the three correlations with the US unemployment rate from 1900 through 2007 are: p < 0.05 for homicide, p < 0.01 for suicide, and p < 0.01 for total violent death rates.

[3] William Julius Wilson, *When Work Disappears: The World of the New Urban Poor*, New York: Vintage, 1996, p.22.

whether the overall rate of unemployment is high or low. The truth of the old adage, "Last to be hired, first to be fired," is thus more than confirmed by the statistics, which also helps to clarify why the homicide rate is so much higher in the black community than in the white.

Unemployment rates are not the only socio-economic variable that predicts changes in suicide and homicide rates. In a study of the relationship between income inequality and violent crime, Hsieh and Pugh[4] performed a meta-analysis of some 34 studies exploring this relationship and found that both (absolute) poverty and income inequality (relative poverty) are significantly correlated with homicide, not just in the United States but throughout the world. Richard Wilkinson[5] has for many years been documenting the relationship between inequality and violence (and many other threats to health) by showing a significant correlation between the incidence of violence and various measures and types of economic inequality and distress, both from his own research and from reviews of the literature produced by other investigators.

---

[4] Ching-Chi Hsieh and M. D. Pugh, "Poverty, Income Inequality, and Violent Crime: A Meta-Analysis of Recent Aggregate Data Studies," *Criminal Justice Review*, 18: 182–202, 1993; reprinted as ch. 26 in Ichiro Kawachi, Bruce P. Kennedy, and Richard G. Wilkinson, eds., *The Society and Population Health Reader*, Vol. I: *Income Inequality and Health*, New York: The New Press, 1999, pp. 278–96.

[5] Richard Wilkinson and Kate Pickett, *The Spirit Level: Why Greater Equality Makes Societies Stronger*, New York: Bloomsbury Press, 2009, especially ch. 10: "Violence: Gaining Respect," pp. 129–44; Richard Wilkinson, "Why is Violence More Common Where Inequality is Greater?" pp. 1–12 in *Youth Violence: Scientific Approaches to Prevention*, Vol. 1036, *Annals of the New York Academy of Sciences*, ed. John Devine, James Gilligan, Klaus A. Miczek, Rashid Shaikh, and Donald Pfaff, 2004.

Another review article observed that "the vast majority of studies of income inequality and homicide rates have employed cross-sectional designs." [6] The shortcoming of that approach is that it leaves the question of what is causing what ambiguous: in a population with a high degree of income inequality, is the increased rate of homicides occurring only among those who are relatively poor, or among the rich, or among both? And if it is primarily caused by the poor, is that because their homicidal behavior is being caused by their poverty, or is their poverty itself caused by the same personality characteristics that make them more likely to commit murder, like being so angry, threatening, and unpleasant to be around that their bosses want to fire them and no one else wants to hire them?

That is why longitudinal studies, such as the ones presented in this book, are more useful for purposes of clarifying the causal mechanisms responsible for these correlations. A study by LaFree and Drass[7] shows the advantages of this approach. They did a time-series analysis of the US from 1957 to 1990 that found that increases in economic inequality were followed by increases in homicide rates (for both blacks and whites). In other words, the same population that had *not* been committing homicides in all the years *before* the state

[6] Steven F. Messner and Richard Rosenfeld, "Social Structure and Homicide," pp. 27–41 in M. Dwayne Smith and Margaret A. Zahn, eds., *Homicide: A Sourcebook of Social Research*, Thousand Oaks, CA, London, and New Delhi: SAGE Publications, 1999, p. 30.

[7] Gary LaFree and K. A. Drass, "The Effect of Changes in Intraracial Income Inequality and Educational Attainment on Changes in Arrest Rates for African Americans and Whites, 1957 to 1990," *American Sociological Review*, 61: 614–34, 1996.

of the economy changed suddenly began doing so only *after* there was a recession, millions of people were laid off from their jobs (regardless of their individual personality characteristics or the quality of the work they were doing), and so on.

In a study of inequality and violent crime (including homicide) sponsored by the World Bank, Fajnzylber, Lederman and Loayza[8] studied the relationship between homicide rates and two related economic variables, income inequality and changes in gross demographic product (GDP), in 39 countries around the world, and concluded that homicide rates are positively correlated with inequality rates and negatively correlated with GDP both within countries and between countries: that is, higher levels of inequality were associated with higher homicide rates, and increasing GDP levels with lower homicide rates. They also concluded that their data provided evidence that inequality was causing violent crimes, not the other way around, and that the combination of decreasing unemployment and rising GDP reduced both absolute and relative poverty, with both changes leading to lower homicide rates.

Land, McCall, and Cohen[9] studied the correlation between six economic variables and homicide rates in cities and states across the United States in 1960, 1970, and 1980, and found that the strongest and most consist-

[8] Pablo Fajnzylber, Daniel Lederman, and Norman Loayza, "Inequality and Violent Crime," *Journal of Law and Economics*, 45: 1–40, 2002.
[9] Kenneth C. Land, Patricia L. McCall, and Lawrence E. Cohen, "Structural Covariates of Homicide Rates: Are There Any Invariances across Time and Social Space?" *The American Journal of Sociology*, 95(4): 922–63, Jan., 1990, p. 951.

ent one was between poverty (both relative and absolute) and homicide: "cities, metropolitan areas, or states that are more deprived have higher homicide rates, and those that are more affluent have lower rates."

Inequality of wealth is even greater than income inequality in the United States, and may also predict rates of lethal violence. The two periods in the United States in which, according to Edward N. Wolff,[10] inequality of wealth – as measured by both household wealth (including home ownership) and financial wealth (including ownership of stocks, bonds, cash, and other fungible resources) – reached its maximum, were both periods in which the lethal violence rate was consistently at epidemic levels. These were the period just before the Great Depression (the degree of inequality of wealth peaked in 1929), and the 1980s, during the Reagan and first Bush administrations, during which time wealth inequality reached the highest level since 1929, and recessions became deeper and unemployment higher than at any time since the Great Depression. Conversely, the quarter of a century from 1942 to 1968 (from Roosevelt's third term in office until the "New Deal Consensus" was ended by the conservative backlash that brought Nixon to power in 1969) was a period of the greatest economic equality of the twentieth century, *and* it was also, as we have already seen, marked by the longest uninterrupted period of well-below-average, non-epidemic lethal violence rates in the twentieth century.

[10] Edward N. Wolff, *Top Heavy: The Increasing Inequality of Wealth in America and What Can Be Done about It* (An Expanded Edition of a Twentieth Century Fund Report), New York: The New Press, 1996.

Finally, my own analysis of economic contractions (recessions and depressions, periods of declining GDP) has found statistically significant relationships between those economic conditions and rising rates of suicide and homicide. As we have already seen, the highest suicide rates (17 per 100,000) and the highest total lethal violence rates (26.5) of the century were reached in 1932, during the bottom of the worst economic depression in our history. That was also when the highest homicide rates ever recorded up to that time occurred (9.5 per 100,000). But even higher murder rates, the highest of the twentieth century, 10.8 and 10.9 per 100,000, were reached three times during the longest period of Republican hegemony of the century, the 24 years from 1969 through 1992. That was a period marked by repeated recessions lasting a total of nearly five years, some of which were deeper than any seen since the 1930s; by unemployment rates that reached levels not seen since the 1930s; and by increases in inequalities in wealth and income that had also not been seen since 1929 (i.e., during the last previous period of extended Republican hegemony that extended from 1921 through 1932). This period of extended and repeated economic stress and distress that occurred during five Republican terms in office (with the most socially and economically conservative Democrat of the century, Carter, sandwiched in between them) was also, as we saw in chapter 1, a time during which there was an extended and uninterrupted "mountain range" of suicide and homicide rates that never once dropped below epidemic levels. So we have good reason to think of those three inter-related economic variables

– unemployment, recessions, and inequality – as being risk factors for lethal violence.

The association between suicide and unemployment has been confirmed repeatedly in dozens of studies, and I think it is fair to say that there is a general consensus now among social scientists as to the validity of this correlation. Many studies have found equally powerful correlations between homicide and unemployment, though these findings have been less consistent than those for suicide. This book is not the place for a full review of the extensive literature on this subject.[11] In line with the majority of the published evidence, my own analysis of the database on which this book is based – which covers the longest time-period and the largest population of any study of this subject – along with that of Dr. Bandy Lee, my research partner, who performed a time series analysis of the data, showed that the correlation between the political parties in power and the violent death rates could be mediated, or caused, by changes in the unemployment rate and in the per-capita GDP (one measure of economic contractions and expansions) that occurred under the two different parties. That leads me to turn to the next step in solving the mystery about murder and its association with the political party ruling the country: is there a relationship

---

[11] For those interested in pursuing this literature further, Chiricos reviewed 63 studies, and concluded that the studies with negative findings were far outweighed, both numerically and on methodological grounds, by those that found statistically significant positive correlations between unemployment rates and homicide rates. See Theodore G. Chiricos, "Rates of Crime and Unemployment: An Analysis of Aggregate Research Evidence," *Social Problems*, 34(2): 187–212, April 1987.

between political parties and the three economic variables I have focused on in this chapter: unemployment, inequality, and recessions?

3

Nothing Succeeds Like Failure

Long before the most vehement critic of capitalism, Karl Marx, was even born, the chief philosophic supporter of capitalism, Adam Smith, noticed that one flaw in this economic system is that the laws of supply and demand make it to the advantage of employers to operate in an economic system that can create a large unemployment rate, because that lowers the "cost of labor," i.e., the wage the employer will need to pay people in order to induce them to work for him. The worst effect of this system is that it turns the laborer – who is, after all, a person with needs and feelings of his or her own – into a commodity, a carrier of labor power that can be bought and sold, and which can be more or less expensive to the employer. Consequently, the political party that is more supportive of and supported by employers (capital) than employees (labor) will have a vested interest in pursuing policies that have the effect of increasing the unemployment rate. This is one of the ways they serve their constituency, whose identity was "outed" by President George W. Bush when he addressed them as "the haves and the have mores."[1]

Inequality, unemployment, and recessions

In comparing the economic performance of Republican and Democratic administrations over the past century, we see a polarization at least as great as that with respect to their effects on rates of lethal violence. Despite presenting itself as the party of prosperity, the Republican party throughout this time has had the effect, as I will show in this chapter, of increasing both the rate and the duration of unemployment, the frequency, depth, and duration of economic contractions (recessions and depressions), and inequalities of income and wealth, meaning increases in the size of the gap between the rich and the poor. They have also, relative to the Democratic party, been far more likely to achieve decreases rather than increases in the median wage, the minimum wage, overall prosperity (the per-capita GDP), and the "Commodification Index" (a measure of the package of benefits provided by the government, including unemployment insurance). As one would suspect, there is a great deal of overlap among these various measures in that they all tend to reinforce each other. For example, recessions increase the unemployment rate, and, as James

---

[1] "This is an impressive crowd – the haves and the have-mores. Some people call you the elites; I call you my base": CBS News, "Bush and Gore do New York," Oct. 18, 2002. Downloaded from www.cbsnews.com/stories/2000/10/18/politics/main24220.shtml.

Galbraith[2] observed, "when unemployment is high, inequality rises. And when unemployment is low, inequality tends to fall." Indeed, he shows mathematically that,

> movements of unemployment alone account for 79 percent of all variation in wage inequality. . . . Other forces are to be reckoned with . . . but changes in unemployment are overwhelmingly the main thing. . . . Nothing else in our history has had a comparable effect. . . . For those who are concerned with inequality, it should be an article of policy that unemployment be kept below the value at which it begins to lead to increased inequality.[3]

Galbraith then goes on to show how both unemployment and its close relative, inequality, dramatically increased during certain periods between 1920 and 1998 and diminished in others. He does not make the connection, but the years during which unemployment and inequality increased so markedly were those when Republican presidents occupied the White House, and the periods of diminishing unemployment and inequality occurred during Democratic administrations. A clear implication of Galbraith's argument, however, is that the unemployment rate can almost be used as a proxy for inequality, or, more simply, as a way of measuring it.

On a personal level, the moment one loses one's job, one experiences an increase in economic inequality between oneself and those who still have jobs. In this sense, the rate and duration of unemployment can be seen as another measure of economic inequality or

---

[2] James K. Galbraith, *Created Unequal: The Crisis in American Pay*, New York: The Free Press, 1998, p. 148.
[3] Ibid., pp. 147–9.

relative poverty, except to the extent – minimal in the US compared with all other economically developed nations – that the wages lost by unemployment are compensated for by unemployment benefits.

Unemployment rates and recessions, respectively, have been measured throughout the twentieth century by the Bureau of Labor Statistics and the National Bureau of Economic Research, and tracking these rates and recessions over time reveals that both of these forms of economic loss and distress have increased in frequency, depth, and duration during Republican administrations and decreased under Democratic ones.

I will deal with unemployment first. One of the most remarkable features of the unemployment figures is that both the rate and the duration of unemployment have increased during every Republican administration and decreased under every Democratic one, without a single exception. In other words, when Republicans have left the White House, the unemployment rate has been higher than it was when they entered it, and when Democrats have left, it has been lower than it was when they entered. If we count up the net sum of all the increases that occurred during all the Republican administrations from 1900 through 2008 (the last year of Bush Jr.), we find that the Republicans brought about a cumulative increase of 27.3 percent in the unemployment rate, and the Democrats an almost exactly equal decrease of 26.5 percent. Thus the net cumulative difference between the effect the two parties had on the unemployment rate during that entire period was 53.8 percent.[4]

[4] See table 1 in appendix B.

The Princeton political economist Larry Bartels[5] has found that in the post-war US, from 1948 to 2005, unemployment rates under Republican presidents averaged 30 percent higher than under Democratic presidents (6.26 percent vs. 4.84 percent respectively).

The duration of unemployment has only been measured since 1948, but it has shown the same partisan difference since that time. Without exception, the duration of unemployment has been longer by the time Republicans left the White House than it was when they entered, and shorter when Democrats left than when they entered. Over the period from 1948 through 2003, the Republicans brought about a net cumulative increase of 24.6 weeks of unemployment among those who were unemployed, and the Democrats, a net decrease of 13.6 weeks, for a net difference between the two parties of 38.2 weeks – nearly 9 months.[6]

The increase in the duration of unemployment not only increases the stress of unemployment and the sense of despair, failure, humiliation, rejection, and worthlessness it brings with it, for obvious reasons; it also has another important implication. Because of an important shortcoming in the data collection process by which the Bureau of Labor Statistics measures unemployment rates, people are simply not counted as unemployed once they have remained unemployed for a long time, on the grounds that, since their continuing inability to find a job has left them too discouraged to keep looking

[5] Larry M. Bartels, *Unequal Democracy: The Political Economy of the New Gilded Age*, New York: Russell Sage Foundation, 2007, p. 48, table 2.4.
[6] See table 2 in appendix B.

for work, they are not really unemployed. What that means is that the longer the duration of unemployment, the more extreme is the undercount of the true unemployment rate. And what that in turn means is that as high as the measured and reported unemployment rates were during Republican administrations, they were almost certainly much higher even than those reported rates. Thus the difference between the Republican and Democratic records with regard to unemployment is probably even greater than it appears to be. That conclusion is not an "opinion," as opposed to a "fact." It is a critique of the process by which something is reported to be a fact, namely, the recording of unemployment rates that are almost certainly, according to virtually every labor economist who has studied this matter, serious underestimates of the true rate of unemployment.

How about recessions? Before I began the research for this book, I had heard so many claims from Republican partisans that they were the party of economic growth, as opposed to their rivals, the Democrats, whom they claimed stifled economic growth with high income, capital gains, corporate and "death" (inheritance) taxes, as well as excessive regulations, that I simply assumed that that was true, and that, as with respect to other matters of public interest, you could vote for Democrats only if you thought the other advantages they could bring to the country outweighed the fact that they were bad for the economy and the Republicans were good for it. Therefore I was genuinely surprised – I would even say shocked – to discover that that reputation of the Republican party appears to be the diametrical opposite of what the numbers show. I am referring to the numbers gathered and published by the National Bureau of Economic Research, which is hardly a liberal or left-wing think tank. Its president for many recent years was Martin Feldstein, who has been an economic advisor to a number of conservative Republican presidents. Yet this group has the reputation of being as objective, non-partisan, and economically expert as any single monitor of the US national economy. One of their most important and influential functions is to determine when the country has gone into a period of economic contraction (a recession or depression) or of expansion. I have reviewed their tabulations of contractions and expansions from 1900 through October 2010, as a way of differentiating between opinion and fact. The conventional opinion is that Republicans are the ones to vote for if you want economic growth, whereas Democrats stifle growth. What do the facts show?

What they show is that, from 1900 through October 2010, the country suffered approximately three times as many months of recessions during the times Republicans were governing the country as during the times Democrats were: 246 months (more than 20 years) compared with 86 – a discrepancy that could not have happened by chance more than 1 time out of 10,000. If we qualify that by examining how many months of contractions they had per year in office (since they occupied the White House for 61 years, as opposed to the Democrats' almost 50 years [through Oct. 2010]), we still find a large discrepancy. The Republicans brought us 2.3 times as many months of recessions per year they were in power as the Democrats did. Furthermore, Republican recessions, when they did occur, lasted more than 4 months longer than those that occurred during Democratic administrations: 14.2 months, as opposed to 9.8. So recessions were more than twice as frequent, and lasted 45 percent longer, under Republicans than under Democrats.

Another difference: recessions began during Republican presidencies 17 times, almost 3 times as often as they did during Democratic ones, when they began only 6 times. In addition, Democrats inherited recessions from outgoing Republican administrations 4 times (in 1913, 1933, 1961, and 2009). By contrast, Republicans inherited recessions from Democrats only once throughout the past 111 years, in 1921, after the ending of which they soon initiated 3 recessions of their own, in 1923 (for 14 months), in 1926 (for 13 months), and then the big one, the Great Depression, which they showed themselves incapable of reversing throughout the entire 43 months in which they remained in office, from August 1929 to March 1933. Franklin Roosevelt then immediately reversed it and began a period of economic expansion that lasted uninterruptedly for the next 50 months. It was then interrupted once, for 1 year (May 1937 – June 1938), by Roosevelt's decision to go back to the kinds of economic policies the Republicans had used and continued to advocate, following which he returned to his original strategies and once again succeeded in bringing about an uninterrupted period of expansion that, contrary to much of the conventional misinformation about the ending of the Depression, continued for 42 months (June 1938 – December 1941) even *before* the US entered the Second World War.

To sum up:

1) Recessions began 3 times as frequently during Republican administrations as during Democratic ones (17 vs. 6). These recessions lasted 45 percent longer per recession, and led to 4 times as many years of recession as occurred during those that began under Democrats (more than 20 years vs. fewer than 5 years).

2) Republicans were 4 times as likely as Democrats to "bequeath" a recession that had begun during their own administration to their successors. They did this 4 times, to Wilson, Roosevelt, Kennedy, and Obama, whereas the Democrats did this to their Republican successors only once (in March 1921, a recession that had begun during Wilson's administration).

3) Nearly a third of the total months of recession that occurred during Democratic administrations were the result of recessions they had inherited from their Republican predecessors (27 out of 86), whereas fewer than 2 percent of the total months of recessions that occurred during Republican administrations were the continuation of the 1 recession they inherited from 1 Democrat (4 months out of a total of 242).

4) This implies that the recessions Republicans handed on to their Democratic successors were deeper, more malignant, and harder to "cure" than the relatively milder and shorter-lived single recession that 1 Democrat left his Republican successors. As a result, the 1 recession Republicans inherited from a Democrat, which occurred in 1921, lasted only

4 further months, whereas the 4 recessions that Democrats inherited from 4 different Republican presidents took a combined total of 27 months to end.

5) This implies further that all 17 of the recessions that began during Republican administrations were largely self-caused, as were all 6 of the recessions that began during Democratic administrations; but that the remaining 4 recessions that existed during Democratic presidencies, which led to almost one-third of the total months of recession that occurred during their administrations, were largely caused by the economic policies of their Republican predecessors. For example, virtually no one believes that Roosevelt caused the Great Depression that he inherited in 1933, which began under Republicans in 1929–30, years before he took office. And no one could reasonably believe that Obama caused the Great Recession that he inherited in 2009, which began under a Republican during 2007. The same applies to the Republican-caused recessions that were inherited by Wilson and Kennedy.

6) The alternative hypothesis, that Republicans were simply more skillful in ending the 1 recession they inherited than the Democrats were in ending the 4 they inherited, does not seem to be supported by the following facts:

7) a) A Democratic president, Roosevelt, in fact succeeded in ending the most serious economic contraction in the history of capitalism, the Great Depression of the 1930s – from the time he first entered office he began taking radical emergency

action that had the effect of reversing the contraction into an expansion, a feat that was never matched by, nor ever needed to be matched by, any Republican president (or, for that matter, any other Democrat).

b) Given that the Republicans showed themselves on 17 different occasions to be incapable of preventing even *non-inherited* recessions during their administrations (as opposed to only 6 comparable failures by Democratic presidents), and less capable of ending those recessions, once they had begun (as was most powerfully shown by their inability to reverse the economic contraction called the Great Depression that started in 1929), as speedily as the Democrats did with their own self-caused recessions, it would be difficult to support the proposition that they were capable of ending *inherited* recessions more rapidly than the Democrats were. It seems more likely that the single recession that a Democrat, Wilson, handed on to his Republican successors in 1921 was less severe than the ones that 4 different Republican presidents left to their Democratic successors.

If we look at the opposite effect, and compare the ability of the two parties to bring about economic growth and expansion, we find that during Democratic administrations the economy was expanding 86 percent of the time, as compared to only 66 percent under Republican presidents.

Another way of measuring the differences between the two parties' ability to increase overall US prosperity by bringing about economic growth is to compare the rate at which the per-capita Gross National Product (GNP) showed a net increase during the years each party was in power. As Bartels[7] has shown, between 1948 (the year in which this concept was first measured and reported) and 2005, the real (inflation-adjusted) per-capita GNP growth rate was 1.64 percent during the years Republicans were in power. What was the growth rate under the Democrats when they were in power? The answer is quite startling: 2.78 percent, which is a full percentage point higher (or, to be more exact, 70 percent higher) than the Republicans' rate, over that 58-year period.

Why has unemployment increased and then lasted longer, and why have recessions occurred so much more frequently and then lasted longer, during Republican administrations than during Democratic ones? And why have declines in unemployment and growth of the economy been so much greater when there was a Democratic president rather than a Republican in the White House? Is this simply a matter of bad luck for the Republicans and good luck for the Democrats? Is it a function of the "business cycle" that operates independently of human political choices, like a force of nature or an act of God that just happens to coincide with times when Republicans are presidents? A misfortune, to be sure, but not their fault?

As opposed to that supposition, many experts on the relationship between the political parties and the

---

[7] Bartels, *Unequal Democracy*, pp. 48–9 (including table 2.4 and figure 2.3).

functioning of the economy have concluded that the latter is very much a function of the difference between the economic policies of the two parties. This has been shown, for example, with respect to why economic inequality increases under Republicans and decreases under Democrats. Writing in 2007, the Princeton political economist Larry Bartels[8] concluded that:

> The most important single influence on the changing US income distribution over the past half-century [has been] the contrasting policy choices of Democratic and Republican presidents. Under Republican administrations, real income growth for the lower- and middle-income classes has consistently lagged well behind the income growth rate for the rich – and well behind the income growth rate for the lower and middle classes themselves under Democratic administrations.

Furthermore, Bartels observes that "these substantial partisan disparities in income growth ... are quite unlikely to have occurred by chance.... Rather, they reflect consistent differences in policies and priorities between Democratic and Republican administrations."

Bartels also points out that one measure of inequality, "the 80/20 income ratio, increased under each of the six Republican presidents in this [post-World War II] period.... In contrast, four of five Democratic presidents – all except Jimmy Carter – presided over declines in income inequality. If this is a coincidence, it is a very powerful one."[9] He then goes on to show reasons why it "seems hard to attribute this to a mere coincidence in

[8] Ibid., p. 30.
[9] Ibid., p. 36.

the timing of Democratic and Republican administrations."

To extend the argument, the political economist Douglas Hibbs[10] points out that "Democratic administrations are more likely than Republican ones to run the risk of higher inflation rates in order to pursue expansive policies designed to yield lower unemployment and extra growth." Hibbs notes that "six of the seven recessions experienced since [1951] . . . occurred during Republican administrations. Every one of these contractions was either intentionally created or passively accepted . . . in order to fight inflation." The cruelest irony of all, in this regard, is that from 1948 through 2005 the inflation rate during Republican administrations has been virtually indistinguishable from that achieved under Democratic ones (3.76 percent vs. 3.97 percent), while the degree of overall prosperity (real per capita GNP growth per year) has been 70 percent higher under Democrats than under Republicans (2.78 percent vs. 1.64 percent), as Bartels[11] has documented. So, while the Republicans have pursued economic policies that have increased unemployment, recessions, and inequality, all ostensibly in order to prevent inflation, they have not in fact succeeded in preventing inflation noticeably better than the Democrats have.

In an analysis of the relationship between recessions and unemployment, Theodore Chiricos has pointed out that, beginning in the 1970s,

---

[10] Douglas Hibbs, *The American Political Economy: Macroeconomics and Electoral Politics*, Cambridge, MA: Harvard University Press, 1987, p. 218.

[11] Bartels, *Unequal Democracy*, pp. 48–9.

unemployment rose more sharply and to higher levels than at any time since the 1930s. In 1969, civilian unemployment reached a fifteen year low of 3.5 percent. Then, three consecutive recessions pushed unemployment to progressively higher levels in 1971 (5.9 percent), 1975 (8.5 percent) and 1982 (9.7 percent). By the spring of 1982, unemployment topped 11 percent in six states. Hardest hit were teenagers, young adults, minorities, and blue-collar workers. For example, unemployment during 1982 reached 14 percent for 20–24-year-old adults, 18 percent for construction workers, 28 percent for auto workers, and 42 percent for black teenagers. By the spring of 1982, fears of economic depression were openly discussed in the national media.[12]

What he did not point out was that these years of increasing unemployment were all years in which Republicans occupied the White House. For example, 1969 was precisely the first year of the new Republican hegemony that replaced the New Deal Consensus that had ruled Washington for the previous 36 years. As a result, "unemployment climbed to levels unmatched in 40 years," i.e., since the last period of Republican hegemony that ended in the Great Depression. Again without mentioning the political parties involved, or the partisan ideological identification of the economists and commentators to whom he refers (such as Martin Feldstein, Milton Friedman, William Safire, James Q. Wilson, and Richard Herrnstein), he points out that, even as this economic disaster was unfolding,

---

[12] Theodore G. Chiricos, "Rates of Crime and Unemployment," p. 187.

the significance of this trend was being discounted in a variety of ways. For example, government economists periodically redefined the concept of "full employment" to include progressively higher levels of unemployment. Some argued that the "new unemployment" was less harmful because it increasingly involved women, teenagers, and voluntary job leavers. Others argued that high unemployment was unavoidable and necessary to combat inflation, or would soon be diminished by the growth of jobs in service industries. Still others claimed that rising unemployment had little or no impact on rates of crime.[13]

And yet, of course, as we have already seen, these were precisely the years when the US entered into the most prolonged epidemic of homicide and suicide of the twentieth century.

Referring to a more recent period, Daniel Hojman and Felipe Kast[14] have shown that during the 1990s (the decade when Clinton was president), significantly fewer people entered poverty and more escaped it than during the 1980s, the Reagan–Bush years.

As I mentioned in the last chapter, the unemployment rate by itself (independent of which party was in power) from 1900 through 2007 correlated positively with changes in all three of the violent death rates that have been measured during that time, to a statistically significant degree ($p < 0.05$ for homicide, $p < 0.01$ for suicide, and $p < 0.01$ for total violent death rates). A time series

[13] Ibid.

[14] Daniel Hojman and Felipe Kast, "On the Measurement of Income Dynamics," Harvard University, Kennedy School Working Paper, Oct. 2009.

analysis performed by Dr. Bandy Lee showed that the effect of the political party in power on violent deaths could be largely explained by the unemployment rate change. Since the parties themselves determine the unemployment rate, however, it is clear that what we have here is a causal circle or an interaction between causal mechanisms, not a reduction to one "true" cause and the elimination of bogus ones. If Republican politicians cause the unemployment rate to rise and the rise in the unemployment rate causes the violent death rates to rise, then it is clear that the Republican party is as responsible as, say, the man who pulls the trigger of the gun, even though it is the bullet not the man that kills the victim.

But a further refinement can be made, indicating that it is not the party label per se that is important but rather the policies of the politician who becomes a Republican president. And here the example of Eisenhower is invaluable. Eisenhower was nominally a Republican president, but he endorsed and supported many of the policies and values that are identified with the Democrats, such as the largest expansion of social security and unemployment benefits since those programs were begun, continuation of the highest marginal income tax rates in our history (91 percent), enforcement of the Supreme Court's desegregation decision, and the promotion of the Department of Health, Education, and Welfare to cabinet status. As a result, many conservative politicians felt that Eisenhower was not one of them (just as Eisenhower himself often felt alienated from the Republican party, on more than one occasion talked of changing parties, and explicitly declared his determination to continue the social and economic policies of

Roosevelt's New Deal). For example, the late William Buckley, whom many people credit with the success of the modern conservative movement that was responsible for the huge Republican gains made throughout the country (from state houses to the Congress) from 1966 to the present, refused to support Eisenhower. And the late Barry Goldwater based much of his campaign to turn the Republican party to the far right on what he claimed was the necessity to move it away from what it had become under Eisenhower.

Just as Eisenhower was the one Republican who did not increase the low rates of lethal violence that he had inherited from his Democratic predecessor, Truman, Jimmy Carter was the one Democrat who did not end the epidemic of violent death that he had inherited from his Republican predecessors, Nixon and Ford. In a recent analysis of the Carter presidency, Hacker and Pierson[15] have pointed out that in many ways Carter's economic policies were more conservative even than Nixon's had been. And just as Eisenhower fantasized about switching to the Democratic party, Carter talked about feeling more comfortable with the Republicans than with his fellow Democrats. And just as many of Eisenhower's fellow Republicans regarded him as not "one of them," so many of Carter's fellow Democrats felt the same way about him. Arthur Schlesinger Jr., for example, as well as many labor leaders, called Carter a Republican and refused to support him. Ultimately, it is policies,

---

[15] Jacob Hacker and Paul Pierson, "The Unseen Revolution of the 1970s," pp. 95–115 in *Winner-Take-All Politics: How Washington Made the Rich Richer – And Turned Its Back on the Middle Class*, New York: Simon and Schuster, 2010.

not party, that determine both economic and behavioral outcomes. The reason the latter are almost always associated with one party or the other would appear to be because the policies of each of the two parties have almost always differed in the same ways from those of the other party. And when that is not true – and only when that is not true – the parties achieve results (or failures) that are otherwise associated with the other party.

Our mystery deepens, although not about murder for the moment. According to the most objective and reliable data that we have concerning prosperity and public safety, the Republican party is the party of poverty and violent death. And yet Republicans regularly come to power by claiming that they are the party of prosperity and public safety. Their failure to succeed in achieving prosperity and decreasing the rates of lethal violence, however, benefits the very constituency to which they appeal, for reasons I will discuss below.

Why the President? Why not the Congress?

But first, I can imagine your asking me why I am concentrating only on the party of the president, not the partisan make-up of the Congress. Why the presidency? There is no question that Congress plays or can play a role with respect to matters of prosperity and public safety. For example, during Johnson's last two years in office (1967–8), the Republican Congressional opposition was sufficiently powerful to block all further progressive civil rights legislation. But it is also true that, to everyone's surprise, the 1994 Republican majority in

Congress was outfoxed by Clinton's brilliant political skills and was unable to stop the passage of many progressive laws and policies.

As the Clinton example illustrates, for the most part the data do not support the notion that Congress influences violent death rates in this country with anything approaching the magnitude, consistency, and statistical significance that the president does. The evidence for the most part supports the position that the president usually wields far more power than the Congress with respect to the matters I am considering here. In any event, the statistical regularities I have uncovered – the correlations between Republican administrations and increases in violent death rates and between Democratic administrations and decreases in violent death rates – are associated with presidential party affiliation (with only two exceptions), not with the partisan majority in Congress.

This same conclusion was reached by Larry Bartels[16] in his studies of the relationship between the political parties in power and rates of unemployment and other forms of economic distress and inequality: he found that the president is far more important in influencing these variables than the Congress is. When Congress does have an effect, it is more likely to consist of stopping the president from doing what he wants to do than of forcing him to do something he does not want to do (which he can usually prevent in any case by means of his veto power).

In short, whether we can explain it comprehensively or not (and I do not pretend to have done so in this short

---

[16] Bartels, *Unequal Democracy*, pp. 34–6.

discussion), it appears, on the basis of the empirical evidence, that the political affiliation of the president is a more powerful determinant of the violent death rates in the US than is the partisan identity of the Congress. How can we understand this, if the "separation of powers" in our national polity is truly between separate but equal branches of government?

This paradox might be explained by Schlesinger's observation that the president of the US has become more powerful than the Congress, especially and increasingly since the beginning of the twentieth century. As Schlesinger[17] put it, "the imperial presidency began with the first Roosevelt and was nourished by the second Roosevelt. It burst into full splendor in the days after the second World War." And he quotes Woodrow Wilson's assessment that the president remains "the only national voice," and the presidency "the vital place of action in the system."

Nor are Schlesinger and Wilson the only ones to reach that conclusion, as is shown by Richard E. Neustadt's study, *Presidential Power and the Modern Presidents*.[18] Neustadt quotes with approval, as does Schlesinger in his book, this passage from an analysis called *The Rise and Growth of American Politics*, published in 1898 by another political scientist, Henry Jones Ford:[19]

---

[17] Arthur Schlesinger Jr., *The Imperial Presidency*, Boston: Houghton Mifflin, 1989.

[18] Richard E. Neustadt, *Presidential Power and the Modern Presidents: The Politics of Leadership from Roosevelt to Reagan*, New York: The Free Press, 1990.

[19] Henry Jones Ford, *The Rise and Growth of American Politics*, New York: Macmillan, 1898, ch. 22, p. 185.

The agency of the presidential office has been such a master force in shaping public policy that to give a detailed account of it would be equivalent to writing the political history of the United States. The evidence ... history affords seems conclusive of the fact that the only power which ... defines issues in such a way that public opinion can pass upon them is that which emanates from presidential authority. The rise of presidential authority cannot be accounted for by the intention of presidents; it is the produce of political conditions which dominate all the departments of government, so that Congress itself shows an unconscious disposition to aggrandize the presidential office.

Why do Republicans win elections?

This still leaves a major mystery unsolved: why would the American people continue to vote into power a political party whose presidents expose them to increased rates of inequality (relative poverty) and violence? And secondly, why would that political party and its presidents continue to pursue policies that lead to those outcomes? It may surprise the reader, as it surprised me, to discover that there is a single answer to both questions. But to discover that answer, we must begin by asking a third question: namely, given that we live in a democracy, why is it that 99 percent of the voters in the United States give 1 percent of the population possession of more than 40 percent of the net wealth of the entire country?

The greatest increases in the concentration of wealth in the twentieth century occurred during the Republican administrations of the 1920s, which led to the Great Depression, and during those from the late 1960s into the 1990s (especially during the 1980s, the Reagan years). The polarization of wealth attained by the Republicans during the "Roaring Twenties" was reversed by the New Deal Consensus from 1933 to the late 1960s. This was accomplished by introducing income supplements for the needy (social security, unemployment benefits, etc.) that had not existed before, reducing unemployment, and creating not only a "minimum wage" but also what was in principle a "maximum wage," by raising the highest marginal income tax rates above 90 percent. The result of these and other policies was what some economic historians have called the "Great Compression" in incomes and wealth that occurred during the most prosperous – and also the most economically equal, and the most non-violent – period in American history (at least with respect to domestic or intranational violence), from roughly 1940 to 1970. Once the Republicans returned to power in 1969, however, that period ended, and inequalities in wealth and income once again reached the same – or nearly the same – levels under Reagan as they had in the 1920s (as did the rates of lethal violence). The rate at which inequality was growing slowed down during the Clinton administration in the 1990s to only about a third of the rate at which it had been growing under his Republican predecessors. This may have been because he succeeded in reducing both the rate and the duration of unemployment, and increasing the highest marginal income tax rates, the Earned Income Tax Credit (the negative income tax which gives money to those who are poor despite having a job), the median and minimum wages, and applying other policies whose effect was to redistribute at least a bit of the national collective income and wealth from the rich to the poor. However, the momentum of the forces producing inequity was still so strong that by 1998 the wealthiest 1 percent of US citizens still owned 38 percent of the total household wealth of the country and 47 percent of the total financial wealth. In other words, the richest 1 percent owned nearly 40 percent of the country's real estate and almost half of its money and other liquid assets (stocks, bonds, etc.).[20]

Although we do not have comparable data yet for rates of lethal violence during the last year of the second Bush administration or the first two years of Obama's presidency, we do know something about their economic policies, and their results. First of all, the current "Great Recession" – as it has been called, in acknowledgment of the fact that it is the worst economic failure the US (and perhaps the world) has suffered since the "Great Depression" of the 1930s (a description that would also describe recessions that occurred during the prior Republican administrations of Nixon, Ford, Reagan, and Bush Sr., although this one is even worse) – occurred right on schedule – after one of the most conservative Republican presidents in US history had been in office for seven years. We also know that when Obama cut a deal with Congressional Republicans to extend unemployment benefits for the long-term unemployed, and to renew tax cuts for middle-class and poor

[20] Wolff, *Top Heavy*.

families, he spoke of those groups as being taken hostage by the Republicans, who would not agree to help the unemployed and the two lower classes unless the Democrats would agree to continue the comparatively enormous income tax cuts that the Bush administration had given to the extremely rich, and to give even larger cuts in inheritance taxes that would primarily be of benefit only to the wealthiest 1 to 1/10 of 1 percent of the American population.

So the mystery is this: how can the wealthiest 1 percent of the population persuade the other 99 percent to agree to a system that is so clearly biased against their economic interests? The Republican party's solution to the problem of how to persuade a majority of the voters to support the party that increases their relative poverty has been to pit the members of the lower middle class against the very poorest lower class, thus distracting the attention of both classes from the fact that it is the upper class (and the party that represents its interests) that is picking their pockets, not each other. As long as the near-poor are fighting with the very poor, neither will fight against the rich – or, to be more exact, against the whole social and economic system that divides the population into a tiny number of very rich people and a huge number of poor and near-poor.

How do they do this? By perfecting the oldest strategy in politics by which a minority can dominate a majority: as the Roman emperors put it, "divide and conquer." But how do they do that?

One means was what Lyndon Johnson called the "Bourbon strategy" in Southern society and politics. He was referring not to the whiskey but to the wealthy white ruling class in the South, the "Bourbons." He said that it was to the political and economic advantage of the Bourbons that racial discrimination continue in the South, because, as long as it did, the poor whites would have an even poorer group of blacks whom they could look down upon and to whom they could feel superior, thus distracting them from feeling envy and resentment toward the rich whites because of their much greater wealth – a clear example of the "divide and conquer" strategy by which a wealthy minority can dominate and exploit a much larger and poorer majority, even in a governmental system that calls itself a democracy. So, of course, the conservative Republicans' "Southern strategy" (which now means the main-stream Republicans' strategy), which many observers have claimed is more responsible than any other single historical development for bringing them back into power in 1969 after 36 years in the political wilderness, has been based on fighting against racial equality by virtually every means at its disposal, including (but not limited to) the following:

1) The policy of mass incarceration, by which I mean the historically unprecedented seven-fold increase in the US imprisonment rate since the mid-1970s, in response to President Nixon's declaration of a "war on crime," which has imprisoned African-Americans to a disproportionate degree, especially for non-violent violations of drug laws which many studies have shown they break no more frequently than whites do, but for which they are imprisoned much more frequently than whites are. The fact that mass incarceration serves no rational interest in increasing

public safety is demonstrated by the evidence that it is both unnecessary and ineffective as a means for preventing violence, as I discuss elsewhere in this book. The irrational interest this policy serves, however, is very clear: it is a means of re-instituting "white supremacy," after the partial successes of the civil rights movement from 1954 to 1965 threatened to reduce racial inequality by legally prohibiting older methods of enforcing it, such as lynching and racial segregation.[21]

2) The disenfranchisement of millions of African-Americans, most of whom would vote for Democrats if they could vote, by defining them as felons (as just described), and then barring them from voting, often for the rest of their lives. This too is a way of finding a substitute for older ways of maintaining white supremacy that are now legally prohibited, such as disenfranchisement of blacks through "poll taxes" and "literacy tests."

3) Supporting litigation whose purpose is to re-institute racial segregation.

4) Opposing laws whose effect would be to increase racial equality.

But there is another historical development that has also had the effect of dividing and conquering the middle and lower classes – indeed, the poorest 99 percent of the population – to the benefit of the Republican party. That is by pursuing policies whose effect is to raise the level

---

[21] See Michelle Alexander, *The New Jim Crow: Mass Incarceration in the Age of Colorblindness*, New York and London: The New Press, 2010.

of criminal violence. I am not suggesting that increasing the rates of violent and other crimes is necessarily, usually, or ever the conscious intent behind those policies, nor do I regard the intent as particularly relevant here. I am talking about the *effect* these policies have, which is to benefit the Republican party whether they are consciously aware that that is what they are doing or not.

How would increases in the homicide rate divide the poorest 99 percent of the population, to the benefit of the wealthiest 1 percent? The answer is simple: most of the violence that our laws define as criminal is committed by poor people, so when criminal violence increases, members of both the upper and the lower middle classes tend to become frightened of and angry at the lower class, which distracts them from noticing that it is the upper class that is actually expropriating the majority of the country's collective wealth and income.

And while most of the violence that our legal system defines as criminal is committed by poor people, most poor people do not commit violent crimes (or any other kind). But most of the victims of violence are poor people. Therefore, a high violent crime rate also tends to divide the poor from each other – that is, to divide the non-violent and non-criminal majority of the poor from that minority among them that is violent and is immediately threatening to them (such as youth gangs, drug dealers, etc.). The effect this has on the inhabitants of crime-ridden inner-city urban ghettos is to distract them from noticing or caring that tax and other laws are written so as to increase the wealth of those who are already rich, and to do so at the expense of the poor. They are too preoccupied with the need to protect themselves from their violent neighbors.

In presenting this analysis, I am not offering a conspiracy theory. I am not suggesting that there is a committee of the Republican party or of the "ruling class" that meets every Monday morning to decide how they can increase the rate of violent crime that week. I am simply describing the way the economic system works of its own volition, so to speak, when the tax laws and other regulations are written so as to benefit the Republican party's main constituency, the super-rich.

What I am describing here is not a conspiracy, it is a conflict of interest. In fact, there are two conflicts of interest, an economic one and a political one. Between whom and whom? First of all, between the *economic* interests of the richest 1 percent of the American population (and the political party that represents their interests), and the interests of the other 99 percent. We know that increases in economic inequality lead to increases in homicide and suicide. But we also know that increases in economic inequality are in the interest of the very rich by definition, because that is what inequality means. When the gap in wealth and income between the rich and the poor increases, what that means is that the rich are getting a larger share of the country's collective income and wealth, and the poor, a smaller share. Thus there is an objective conflict of interest between the *economic* interest the richest 1 percent of the country has in becoming even richer, and the interest the other 99 percent have in living in a less violent society, as well as the interest they have in gaining access to a larger share of the country's collective wealth and income.

As I said, the main victims of violent crime are the poor, and an increase in the rate of criminal violence offers minimal threat, if any, to the rich, who live in gated communities or are otherwise protected by expensive security arrangements. One of the more astonishing facts about the United States today is that more money is spent on private security forces for the rich than on police forces and other security arrangements for the rest of the population.

But there is also another conflict of interest here: a *political* one. It is in the political interest of the very rich for the country to have high rates of violent crime, since the higher the crime rate, the more the voting population is able to be divided and conquered, as the high crime rate alienates the middle class from the poor, and the poor from each other – the non-violent majority from the violent minority by whom they feel most directly and immediately endangered. When that happens, the middle classes are less likely to vote for the party that identifies itself with the interests of the poor (who are seen as violent and dangerous); and the poor are less likely to vote for the party that is less punitive toward the criminals (since they have been misled into believing that increasing the amount of punishment will reduce the rate of violence, rather than increase it). Since both poverty and violence are concentrated among easily identifiable racial and ethnic groups, the Republican party has been able to play on the fears of poor and lower-middle-class voters from majority racial and ethnic groups who feel threatened by those who belong to minority groups.

The higher the rates of crime and violence, then, the

more that members of the middle and lower classes become manipulated into fighting against each other, and distracted from noticing that the people by whom they are most in danger of being robbed are not the relatively small number of armed robbers among them, but the even smaller number of very wealthy people and their agents, the Republican politicians who write the laws that divert money into their hands and out of the hands of the lower and middle classes. As the old saying goes, the poor man robs you with a gun, the rich man with a pen.

In advocating policies that increase the level of social and economic stress and distress to unbearable levels, and thus increase the rates of suicide and homicide, the Republican party succeeds in winning elections precisely by failing to achieve its stated goals of prosperity and public safety. Thus "nothing succeeds like failure."

In this analysis, I am not assuming that many individual members of any of these classes – the upper, middle, or lower – are actually consciously aware of the role they are playing in this conflict. Some in each class are aware of it, and, of those who are, some work consciously to support this system and some work consciously to oppose it. But the beauty of the system, from the standpoint of the interests of the rich, is that the vast majority of people whose lives are affected by it, whether for good or for ill, do not have to understand the system or consciously support it in order for it to work. The socio-economic and criminal justice systems themselves do that job for them, so that individuals do not have to do anything different from what they have always done for the system I have just described to work and perpetuate and reproduce itself. Simply maintaining the status quo, individual by individual, maintains the status quo for the social system as a whole.

Representative strategists in both major American political parties are aware of these facts, and use them consciously in devising their political strategies. For example, Barry Goldwater's campaign manager in 1964 said that crime in America was a free, multi-million-dollar gift to the Republican party, and, as the senior President Bush's campaign strategist Lee Atwater put it, "Crime was a 'wedge issue' to be driven into the Democratic party in order to fragment it."[22] In other words, Divide and Conquer!

And Democratic strategists are fully aware not only that this is the strategy of the very wealthy, but that it has been a very powerful and largely successful strategy. As the Democratic representative Barney Frank said, "There is an important political imperative: for the Republicans not to be able to accuse the Democrats of being soft on crime. Period. We have a dilemma – division within the party."[23] Again, divide and conquer. And as Senator Charles Schumer put it, referring to the Republican party strategists, "they want a lot of criminals. The Republican party only succeeds when the race issue is the divide . . . When they try to win on non-race – abortion, gays – they lose. That's why they're going to crime . . . That's when they win. They know it."[24]

Perceptive social scientists have long known this. As Christopher Jencks[25] put it:

[22] Sidney Blumenthal, "Crime Pays," *The New Yorker*, May 9, 1994, p. 44.
[23] Ibid.
[24] Ibid.
[25] Ibid., p. 33

Like rain on election day, crime is good for the Republicans. Whenever crime seems to be increasing, significant numbers of Americans tend to blame liberal permissiveness and turn to conservative political candidates, partly because they endorse a sterner approach to raising children, policing the streets, and punishing criminals, and partly because they oppose government "give aways" to the poor – blacks and other groups that commit a lot of crimes. While orthodox liberals answer that "getting tough" won't really help and that the way to reduce crime is to make society more just and opportunity more equal, this response to crime has seldom moved the electorate. When crime rates rise, liberals almost always find themselves on the defensive.

And, as Edgar Z. Friedenberg[26] wrote, it is important

to demonstrate the ways in which crime *does* pay – not for criminals but for certain elements in the community at large . . . For dominant social groups, it is an epiphenomenon that is costly mostly to lesser people whose lives are not so well guarded, a side effect of the operation of the kinds of values that have made our capitalism effective. Eliminate violent crime? We couldn't leave home without it!

The true brilliance of the Republican party's strategy is that the real interests which that strategy is serving, and the means by which it serves them, are concealed by a rhetoric that states the strategy is serving exactly the opposite interests and pursuing exactly opposite goals from those that it is actually serving and pursuing. And despite the fact that Orwell anatomized this rhetoric

[26] Ibid.

with the utmost clarity in his concept of "double speak," it still deceives millions of voters. Thus, instead of openly acknowledging that it is in the interest of the rich to have a high crime rate, the political rhetoric of the Republican party claims to want to decrease the rate of violence.

But the brilliance of this strategy does not end there. For it also includes a corresponding form of double speak – namely, labeling those policies that would actually decrease the rates of violence as being "soft on crime." That is how "the Republicans have used the law and order issue for a generation to kneecap Democrats at will," as Sidney Blumenthal put it; "From the election of Richard Nixon through the election of George Bush, the Republicans held a strategic advantage on crime which was the domestic political equivalent of their advantage in foreign policy."[27] Without a high crime rate, in other words, the Republican party would lose one of its major political advantages, one of its strongest vote-capturing issues – "the war on crime," "law and order," "getting tough on crime," and so on.

It would take another George Orwell to do justice to the irony in the fact that it is precisely the failure of the Republican party to diminish criminal violence that is responsible for its success in dividing and conquering the electorate; and it is precisely the failure to create prosperity and diminish poverty that is responsible for the elevated crime rate which is responsible for Republicans' electoral victories. In other words, the motto of the Republican party is, in effect, "nothing succeeds like failure." The more they fail at

[27] Ibid.

providing prosperity and public safety, the more they succeed.

Thus, we are able to answer the question: if Republican administrations do in fact elevate violent death rates, and if practically none of those who vote for a Republican president in any particular election has the slightest desire to bring about that outcome (an assumption that I will simply take for granted), then why do people vote for Republicans? When investigating crime and corruption, the Roman lawyer Cicero asked: *Cui bono* – Who benefits? If Republicans regularly bring about epidemics of lethal violence once they come into power, we similarly can ask: who benefits? For it is hard to imagine that a political party would continue to repeat the same manifestly destructive policies unless it, and the interest groups it was serving and being supported by, were in some way benefiting from them. I have suggested that this question can be answered not by assuming some complicated conspiracy theory, but rather by noticing the simple and obvious conflicts of interest that exist between the Republican party's main constituency (the richest 1 percent of the population), and the interests of the other 99 percent of the population.

We all know what conflicts of interest are, and why we have laws against them. It is not that people always sacrifice the public interest in favor of their private interest when they are faced with such a conflict. Indeed, some of the very rich fight against the inequities in our political and economic system more vigorously than do most of us who are less well-off. I am thinking here of people like Franklin Delano Roosevelt, who was called a "traitor to his class," though it would be more accurate to say that he was a traitor to a class system that deserved no loyalty – indeed, that was a central part of his greatness. In the contemporary world, George Soros has generously lavished his considerable fortune on groups that fight to increase political and social democracy both in the United States and around the world. But we also know that, human nature being what it is, most people are not Franklin Roosevelt or George Soros, and, when faced with a conflict of interest, will often sacrifice the public interest to their own private interest, which is why we outlaw such conflicts (when we do).

How (and why) to increase the level of violence

The main obstacle to preventing violence is not lack of knowledge as to how to do it; rather, it is lack of the political will to make the changes in our society that would prevent violence, or, in other words, lack of the political will to discontinue the policies that cause violence. This simple fact has been largely obscured by a great deal of political propaganda whose effect is to persuade people that policies that stimulate violence actually prevent it, and that policies that prevent it actually stimulate it. Another way to say this would be to point to a paradox: although most voters and most politicians claim to want to diminish the level of violence in the world, they repeatedly pursue policies whose effect is to increase the frequency and intensity of violence. How can we understand this paradox? For unless we can learn how to understand it and to discontinue this self-defeating behavior, we will never be able to implement the policies that we now know are both necessary and sufficient for the prevention of violence.

What do I mean by self-defeating behavior that stimulates violence rather than preventing it? For the sake of brevity, I will mention only a few particularly egregious examples, though one could easily come up with a list of dozens.

1) Among the only drugs we know of that actually inhibit, and thus can be said to prevent, violence, two of them, marijuana and heroin, have been declared illegal and their use has been made punishable by increasingly severe prison sentences ever since our first modern Republican president, Richard Nixon, declared his "war on drugs" during his election campaign in 1968. When I say that they prevent violence, I mean exactly that: people who are under their pharmacological influence are less violent than when they are not exposed to the effects of these drugs.[28] The only drug that we know of that causes violence (alcohol) is legal, as is the most addictive and deadly of all the drugs of abuse (tobacco). And the main cause of the association between illegal drugs and violence is not the drugs (not even cocaine). It is the

---

[28] Klaus A. Miczek et al., "Alcohol, Drugs of Abuse, Aggression, and Violence," pp. 377–570 in Albert J. Reiss and Jeffrey A. Roth, eds. (Panel on the Understanding and Control of Violent Behavior, National Research Council, National Academy of Sciences), *Understanding and Preventing Violence*, Vol. III, Washington, DC: National Academy Press, 1994. See also, among many excellent studies documenting how counter-productive the "war on drugs" is, Steven B. Duke and Albert C. Gross, *America's Longest War: Rethinking Our Tragic Crusade against Drugs*, New York: G. P. Putnam's Sons, 1993.

criminal justice system itself, i.e., the laws declaring the drugs illegal, which have the effect of providing a multi-billion-dollar, tax-payer-financed subsidy of the various drug cartels throughout the world and the inner-city drug dealers in our own country who engage in violence to increase their share of an illegal drug market which would not exist in the first place if conservative lawmakers had not created it by criminalizing the drugs.

Much careful epidemiological research has shown that the main source of the violence associated with illegal drugs is the war between the different drug dealers and gangs, not violence committed by those currently intoxicated (most of whom become less violent, not more so, as long as they have their drug of choice). And yet this exorbitantly expensive method of stimulating violence is done in the name of preventing violence. The criminalization of these drugs is one of the main causes of violence throughout the world. If they were decriminalized, the drug cartels would go out of business tomorrow, just as the bootleggers did when the prohibition of alcohol in the US was repealed right after Franklin Roosevelt was elected in 1933. Until our legislators do this, the criminalization of drugs will continue to provide the main source of funding for: (a) the Taliban, Al Qaeda, and other groups, in the fight against whom we have spent an estimated trillion dollars and sacrificed thousands of military and civilian lives; (b) the Mexican drug cartels who have so much money they have been able to corrupt most of the government and purchase weapons more powerful than even the Mexican army can use against them, and thus threaten to turn that country into a failed state unable to defend its own citizens; (c) other drug cartels throughout the world who are so affluent they are able to destabilize whole national governments, for many of whom their GDP is less than the wealth and income of the cartel owners.

While the drugs we have criminalized do not, in and of themselves, cause violent behavior, they can cause medical problems. That is why it would be appropriate to treat their use as a problem in public health, not as a crime. Substance abuse treatment has been shown to be much more therapeutically effective than imprisonment in enabling drug addicts to overcome their addiction, and is vastly less expensive than imprisonment. And yet, because of the Republican-initiated "wars" on "crime" and "drugs," we continue to waste billions of dollars of taxpayers' money, and to turn our country into a virtual police state, with the highest imprisonment rate of any country in the world (including those that actually are police states), by building more and more prisons and overcrowding them with non-violent drug addicts (whom we confine in prisons where they are all too often forced into becoming either victims or perpetrators of violence), rather than offering them the treatment that could actually cure their addiction, by means that would be: (a) less expensive than imprisonment, (b) less cruel than imprisonment, and (c) more therapeutically effective than imprisonment.

2) Earlier in my career, in the 1970s and 1980s, I

headed the Institute for Law and Psychiatry at the Harvard Medical School. In that capacity, I served as Medical Director of the prison mental hospital, as well as of mental health services for all of the state prisons in the Massachusetts Department of Correction. A major responsibility I had was to end an epidemic of violence – i.e., suicides and homicides – in the prison system, since the federal courts that ordered the state to let us provide psychiatric treatment to the prisoners had determined that much of this violence was associated with undiagnosed, untreated, and overwhelming mental and emotional stress and distress.

One year, my colleagues and I investigated which of the various rehabilitative and therapeutic programs available to the prisoners had been most effective in preventing recidivism, or reoffending, among those who left the prison and returned to the community. What we found was that there was one program, and only one, that had been 100 percent effective in preventing recidivism, and that was gaining a college degree while in prison. For 25 years, Boston University professors had been volunteering their time to teach college-credit courses in Massachusetts prisons. Between 200 and 300 prisoners had gained at least a bachelor's degree over a 25-year period, and we found that not one of them had been returned to any prison for a new crime. At first I thought that perhaps we had made a mistake, that perhaps we had missed some, but then we discovered that several other prisons or prison systems had had the same result – zero recidivism in the

Indiana state prison system, 0 percent at the Folsom State prison in California, and so on among those who had gained at least a baccalaureate in prison. Not every prison had such perfect results, of course, and neither did we when we extended the study to 30 years and discovered 2 recidivists over a 30-year period – less than a 1 percent recidivism rate over 30 years, compared to the US rate of 65 percent after only 3 years. Similarly, state prison systems throughout the United States have repeatedly found college education to be not only effective, but the most effective single program capable of reducing recidivism rates.

Now, of course, this was an atypical group of prisoners, clearly more motivated and already more educated than most prisoners. On the other hand, they had committed crimes just as serious as anyone else – murder, rape, etc. And given the prison system's usual scandalously high recidivism rate, it seemed to me that any government official interested in reducing the incidence of violent crime in our communities would immediately do everything possible to increase the availability of college education to every prisoner who had the slightest degree of interest or ability.

Little did I know. When I reported the results of my research on this issue in a lecture series I gave at Harvard, a friend who attended gave a copy of my lectures to our new governor, a Republican Harvard graduate and former prosecutor who had been elected to office on the campaign promise to "reintroduce prisoners to the joys of busting rocks."

He had not realized until then that there was a program of free higher education in the prison system. Within days, he gave a press conference in which he stated that we should abolish this program, or otherwise people who could not afford to go to college would start committing crimes so they could go to prison and get a free college education. And he in fact did succeed in effectively vitiating the program. Nor is this simply the behavior of one politician in one state: three years later, the Republican majority that was elected to the US Congress under Newt Gingrich's leadership in 1994 repealed the federal grant that provided the relatively small amount of funds necessary to pay for college textbooks and tuition for inmates in prisons throughout the country. So, in the name of fighting crime and being tough on criminals, Republican politicians systematically and deliberately dismantled the single most effective program we have yet discovered for enabling people to leave a life of crime and violence. And the "war on crime," as this irrational and self-defeating behavior is called, is just as Orwellian a reversal of the plain meaning of the words of the English language as is the "war on drugs." Indeed, all these slogans have their model in Orwell's *1984*: "War is peace," "slavery is freedom," etc.

3) Studies have repeatedly found that when juveniles (children under the age of 18) are sent to adult prisons, not only are they more likely to be raped and to commit suicide, but also those who survive long enough to be released from these prisons reoffend at higher rates and commit more violent offenses

than when they are sent to juvenile detention centers and housed with other children. Yet many state legislatures have passed laws mandating the transfer of juveniles to adult prisons. They do not say that their purpose is to raise the rates of violence and recidivism to the highest possible level, but that is the effect of the laws they have been passing.

4) Studies consistently show that the more severely children are punished, the more violent they become. Yet our courts and legislatures have continued to authorize the corporal punishment of children, a practice that is most strongly approved of by Republican voters and legislators, and residents of the Republican-dominated "Red States" (as I will discuss in chapter 6).

5) Between 1984 and 1994, the rates of both committing homicide and being a victim of homicide tripled among 14- to 17-year-old American boys. This explosive increase in the murder rate was caused by one weapon and one weapon only – hand guns. Yet the US Congress and virtually every state legislature refuses to outlaw the private possession and use of these weapons, despite the fact that people are far more likely to be killed by whatever guns they have in their own homes (where they cause fatalities in family quarrels, suicides, and so-called accidents) than they are by the guns of criminals invading their homes (a phenomenon so rare it can be considered more of a paranoid fantasy – or delusion – than a reasonably probable reality). The Republican party both supports and is supported by the National Rifle Association, the main lobbying group opposing the banning of hand guns.

I could go on and on, but I think I have made my point: there is a disconnect between what the Republican party says it is doing (preventing violence) and what it is actually doing (stimulating violence).

There are undoubtedly several additional factors that explain the Republican party's surprising degree of electoral success, including the facts that the wealthiest 1 percent of the population owns the mass media which tell people what to think, what to believe, whom to vote for, and so on (as someone said, the press is free – for anyone who owns one), and that the wealthiest individuals and corporations donate a disproportionate percentage of the campaign funds that are the prerequisite for running for office in the United States, so that most politicians – Democrats as well as Republicans – are under tremendous pressure to serve the economic and political interests of the very wealthy.

The politics of suicide

One mystery remains here: how has the public been led to overlook the relationship between suicide and politics? At least a partial answer to this might be that there is another divide and conquer strategy going on here, even if it is completely unconscious – namely, the division between suicide and homicide. Clearly, it is in the interest of conservative political parties to deny, as far as possible – as Margaret Thatcher did – that there is any such thing as society, because society is the arena in which politics exerts its effects. Therefore, if you want to make a political party immune to being accountable for what happens in society as a whole – such as increases in unemployment, recessions, and poverty, or in the rates of either suicide or homicide that those economic stresses increase – you will want to isolate those disasters from the range of events for which the political parties can be held responsible. That is, you will want to claim that the economic system functions according to natural laws that can no more be changed than we can change the laws of gravity, rather than that it is a game that functions according to the laws and rules we write regarding how to play the game. And it is also to the political advantage of the conservative parties whose impact on the suicide rate is only to elevate it (as has been documented, in the United States, the United Kingdom, and Australia, at least), to deny that there is any relationship between what happens in and to "society" – or, in other words, their policies and practices – and the suicide rate. One way to do that is to insist that suicide is a completely personal, individual act which is caused exclusively by an individual's private mental illness or despair, not by public policies or societal trends. The conservative party in the United States, the Republican party, has been all too successful in achieving this goal.

What I find more surprising is the degree to which the social sciences and the mental health professions have sometimes unwittingly colluded in this. To see suicide as an act of violence seems self-evident. From the standpoint of public health and preventive psychiatry, the discovery of the social and environmental causes or risk factors that can lead to epidemics of this form of premature, unnecessary, and often preventable death is of the utmost importance. Tens of thousands of deaths a year in the US alone, and hundreds of thousands around the world, are at stake.

But the moment we take that approach, we threaten those who have a stake in blinding themselves to the impact of social, economic, and political forces on the suicide rate. To see suicide simply as an individual mental illness and homicide as a similarly individual moral failing is to ignore the degree to which both are caused, in part, by social, economic, and political forces. There are many individual factors that can increase or decrease a person's tendency to both suicide and homicide, including heredity, life experience, individual personality structure and the like, but the *epidemics* of both of these forms of lethal violence are clearly caused by changes in the social environment, including economic and political events, rather than by some sudden change in the genome or the personality structure of the tens of thousands of additional people who just happen to decide to commit murder or suicide only after a Republican becomes president.

4

The Shame of It All

None of this can be understood, however, without understanding the individual psychology involved. We cannot understand or explain epidemics of lethal violence without understanding what leads individuals to become violent, since it is individuals, after all, who are the perpetrators of violence, whether their victims are themselves or other people. Whether one reads the story of Cain and Abel or the *Iliad* or the plays of Shakespeare or the daily newspaper, or talks with people who have committed murder, or listens to people who are suicidal, when it comes to violence, all roads lead to shame. In previous publications,[1] I have identified shame as the proximal cause of violent behavior, the necessary – though not sufficient – pathogen, in the same sense that the tubercle bacillus is necessary but not sufficient

---

[1] Gilligan, *Violence*; Gilligan, "Shame, Guilt and Violence"; James Gilligan, "Exploring Shame in Special Settings: A Psychotherapeutic Study," pp. 475–90 in Christopher Cordess and Murray Cox, eds., *Forensic Psychotherapy: Crime, Psychodynamics and the Offender Patient*, Vol. II, London: Jessica Kingsley, 1995.

for the development of tuberculosis. Everybody experiences feelings of shame at one time or another, yet most people never commit an act of serious violence (just as most people exposed to the organism that "causes" tuberculosis do not come down with the disease). Therefore, it is clear that there are other determinants of violent behavior, such as biology, culture, social class, age, sex, and many others. But when violence does occur, experiences of shame and humiliation or the fear of undergoing these experiences, is an ever-present prerequisite.

There is a paradox at the heart of shame. Although we usually think of shame as an emotion, and an extremely painful one at that, the paradox is that shame is actually the absence of an emotion, namely, the emotion of self-love (or, as it is also called, pride, self-respect, self-esteem, or the feeling of self-worth). The power of shame is often overlooked because of the fact that the most painfully shameful experiences are frequently those in which the provocation of shame seems most trivial, objectively. The greatest psychologists are often novelists, and William Faulkner illustrates this point powerfully in his tragic novel about the antebellum South, *Absalom, Absalom*, in which he shows how his protagonist's entire life becomes consumed and ultimately destroyed by his attempt to heal the shame caused by an incident in which, when he was young and penniless, a black slave who was serving as butler to a rich white plantation-owner imperiously and contemptuously orders him to enter by the back door of the mansion, not the front.

Shame is often overlooked because people who feel

ashamed are often ashamed to reveal that they feel ashamed and how ashamed they feel, because it is shameful to feel ashamed, since that implies that one is so weak, incompetent, inadequate or, inferior that one can be shamed – which is more true, the more objectively "trivial" the incident was by which one was shamed. Therefore, the more deeply shamed people feel, the more likely they are to conceal their shame behind a mask of bravado or *braggadocio* – or violence.

People don't have to have had the kind of specialized experiences I have had with both homicidal and suicidal individuals in order to recognize how central shame is to the genesis of violence. For example, every reader of newspapers in the United States read recently the tragic story of a college student who jumped off the George Washington Bridge after some of his classmates secretly filmed him having sex with one of his male classmates, and then posted the video on the internet where everybody could see it.

When I have asked murderers in prisons why they assaulted, or even killed, someone, the answers I have received have been astonishingly similar: "because he (or she) disrespected me." They used the word "disrespect" so often that they abbreviated it into the slang term "he dis'ed me." When people use a word so often that they abbreviate it, that may tell you how central the word is in their moral and emotional vocabulary. But you do not need to go into prisons and talk with murderers in order to know this for yourself. In the book of Genesis, the relation between disrespect and violence is described with utmost clarity in the story of the first recorded murder in Western history, the story of Cain's murder of his brother Abel. The Bible says very clearly why Cain killed Abel; it was because "God had respect unto Abel and unto his offering and unto Cain and his offering God had not respect." In short, God "dis'ed" Cain; or Cain was "dis'ed" because of Abel, and he acted out his anger at being disrespected in exactly the same way as the murderers I saw had done.

People commit homicide and other acts of violence on others in order to undo feelings of shame that are intolerably painful (or to avoid feelings of shame that would have that effect), by transferring their shame from themselves to their victim. By assaulting the other person, they prove that the victim is weaker than they are and therefore more shameful. Our language alone tells us this. Two of the words that we use with which to describe acts of violence are "assault" and "injury." "Assault" comes from the same Latin roots as the word "insult," and, even in English, the word "insult" also has the meaning of a physical assault or injury, as when surgeons refer to an incision as the surgical insult. And "injury" is the English descendant of the Latin word *iniuria*, which means "insult" (it also means "injury," as well as "injustice," and also is used to refer to rape). One does not have to add insult to injury; it is already there, in the word, the feeling, and the act itself. To assault or injure someone is to insult or, in other words, shame them.

But what about suicide, which in many ways is the opposite of homicide? People can also commit suicide as the only means they have available by which to escape from intolerable intensities of shame, even though they might prefer to commit homicide instead if they had the power to do so. Examples would include defeated Japanese Samurai, who would commit the ritual form of suicide called *seppuku* or *hara kiri* as a means of proving their courage and to avoid being executed in a shameful manner, even though their first choice, if they had not been defeated and disarmed, would have been to continue killing the enemy. Likewise, and for much the same reason, Antony and Cleopatra killed themselves (as Cleopatra made clear in her suicide note) in order to avoid the shame of being led through Rome in chains so that Octavian could celebrate his victory over them. While the suicides of many of the violent criminals in prisons today may have analogous motives, the motives of most suicides and suicidal people in the community are, in my experience, not that simple.

To understand suicide more fully, we must also consider another emotion, the feeling of guilt. Guilt is the emotion that motivates self-punishment. The paradox about suicide and guilt is that, while guilt is in some respects the opposite of shame – that is, its causes tend to be the opposite of those that cause shame and the behaviors it motivates tend to be the opposite of those motivated by shame – it nevertheless is inextricably related to shame. Shame motivates active, aggressive behavior toward other people, which can escalate to homicide under certain exceptional circumstances. The psychological function of guilt feelings is to inhibit (i.e., prohibit) the hostility toward others that shame has stimulated, which people can sometimes manage to do only by redirecting their hostile and violent impulses toward themselves instead. Thus, shame can motivate homicide as well as suicide, depending on whether the person believes he can succeed in wiping out his shame by means of violence toward others, or can only put an end to this intolerably painful feeling by killing himself.

However, for people who have developed an internalized conscience and the capacity to feel guilty and remorseful over impulses and wishes to harm others, the motivation for suicide is more likely to involve both shame and guilt. The emotion of guilt consists of anger and aggression that are directed against the self. But the aggression that is the essence of guilt has actually been stimulated by the experience of feeling shamed. Most people, except for psychopaths, have developed at least some capacity to feel guilt and remorse, and have developed an internalized conscience that forbids them from harming other people. When they experience a major shame-provoking event such as being ruined financially, or being fired from their job, or being rejected by a lover or betrayed by a spouse, or losing their home in a foreclosure, they can be expected to experience a steep intensification of anger, which shame always stimulates, but which, because of the power of their conscience and their guilt feelings, they internalize and direct against themselves, sometimes leading to suicide.

This is one way of understanding how the same social and economic stresses, such as unemployment or bankruptcy or homelessness, can lead to increases in the rates of both homicide and suicide, even though the people who respond to these stresses with homicide may have very different personalities and very different motivations from the people who respond to them with suicide. And, not infrequently, as everyone knows who reads the newspapers, those who kill others may go on to kill themselves as well.

We do need to recognize, however, that suicide and homicide are simply the most extreme and least common of all the responses to socio-economic stress. They are the tip of the iceberg, so to speak, underneath which are many times more people who suffer grievously from these stresses but do not respond to them by killing others or themselves. The fact that suicide and homicide rates do increase with a magnitude so great that they look like mountain peaks on a graph becomes an indicator of the degree to which many more people are affected by changes in the political party of the occupant of the White House and the social and economic consequences of these shifts in political party.

Psychodynamically, shame functions as a motive for stifling wishes that are experienced as shameful, such as wishes to be loved and taken care of by others, which may be seen as rendering one passive, dependent, childish, or (for men) "feminine" in nature, as opposed to being an active, self-sufficient, autonomous, and independent adult who takes pride in being able to "take care of himself." The capacity to feel shame can play an adaptive role in human life to the extent that it motivates ambition, maturation, development, achievement, the acquisition of skills and knowledge, and the other prerequisites of autonomy, self-respect, and the capacity to win respect from others. The problem with this, however, is that none of us is ever completely dependent or independent; we are all, always, interdependent. To the extent that people misidentify their own need for help and support from others as a shameful sign of personal failure or weakness rather than a feature of the human condition (as I have sometimes said to my patients, "we all need all the help we can get"), they are likely to project their own need for support onto so-called "welfare queens" whom they can then shame, reject, and punish. That is one way in which shame can stimulate right-wing political and economic attitudes and values. To the shame-driven person, "dependency," such as being dependent on "welfare," is not something to be sympathized with, it is one of the worst evils, something to be shamed, condemned, ostracized, and punished.

But an even more destructive by-product of shame will occur when a person defends against his wish to be "passive and dependent" (i.e., loved and taken care of by others) by going to the opposite extreme, and becomes active and aggressive toward others, even to the point of violence. For example, the health care reforms that were proposed by the current Democratic president, Obama, and passed by the Democrats in Congress over the almost unanimous opposition of Republicans, were responded to in many different parts of the country with death threats against those who had supported this attempt to ensure that the sick would be taken care of. What one sees here is the depth and intensity of a psychology of shame.

Shame ethics vs. guilt ethics

Shame and guilt are the emotions of morality, and therefore also the emotions of politics. To be more exact, they are the emotions of the two antagonistic moral and political value systems that exist in the world – in political terms, "right-wing" vs. "left-wing" ideologies. To understand moral conflict and therefore political conflict, it is absolutely essential to realize that there is not just one morality but two, and not just one politics but two. Despite the fact that morality is often spoken of as though there were only one moral value system, to which people adhere or else they are immoral, the fact is that there have always been two opposite moralities and they have been recognized by moral thinkers from the very beginning of moral and political discourse, which, in the West, at least, means from the time of ancient Greece and Israel.

Shame ethics is a moral value system in which the greatest evil is shame and humiliation, i.e., dishonor and disrespect, and the highest good is the opposite of shame, namely, pride and honor (respect). Guilt ethics is a moral value system in which the greatest evil is guilt (also called sin), and the highest good is the opposite of guilt, namely, innocence. But these two value systems are opposites. For example, in the guilt ethic of Christianity, the worst evil, the deadliest of the seven deadly sins, is pride, which is the highest good in a shame ethic. Thus guilt ethics supports egalitarianism, so that nobody can experience the pride of being superior to others (and no one will be shamed or humiliated by being considered inferior to others), just as shame ethics valorizes a hierarchical social system in which some people are superior and therefore experience pride and honor, meaning that others are inferior and subjected to feelings of inferiority or shame. The guilt-ridden person recognizes that we are all sinners, and that we all stand in need of forgiveness from others for the harms we have done to them, so that it would be utter hypocrisy not to forgive others for the harm they do to us. On the day of Atonement, in the guilt-ethic of Judaism, Jews are called upon to ask forgiveness from those they have offended or sinned against, and a person's failure to forgive after the third request makes him or her guilty of the sin they refused to forgive. The shame-driven person, by contrast, sees revenge as not only permitted but even required, for the failure to revenge yourself on someone who has harmed you (or a member of your family or cultural group) deprives you of "honor."

The opposite of pride is humility, which is a prerequisite for innocence, so that humility is valued as one of the highest goods in a guilt ethic; whereas for a shame ethic, humility is tantamount to self-humiliation, which is the worst evil. One consequence of these value differences is that people who live by a guilt ethic will identify with those of low social status as a way of renouncing pride and embracing humility, whereas people who live by a shame ethic will identify with those of superior social and economic status as a way of enhancing their pride and assuaging their own feelings of shame and inferiority. To put it in everyday English, those who live by a guilt ethic are likely to identify with the underdog, and those who are ruled by a shame ethic have an incentive to identify with the overdog (or the *Ubermensch*, the "superman," in the shame-ethic of Nietzsche – who emphasized that his "master-morality" is the opposite of Jesus' "slave-morality" by identifying himself, in one of his last writings, as "The Anti-Christ").

Political examples of these two different attitudes can

be seen in the contrast between the goals enunciated by Franklin Roosevelt and Ronald Reagan. As Roosevelt put it, "The test of our progress is not whether we add more to the abundance of those who have much; it is whether we provide enough for those who have too little."[2] Reagan, by contrast, said (speaking of the Republican party) that "We're the party that wants to see an America in which people can still get rich."[3] Roosevelt was identifying with the underdog, the person who has too little, and advocating the reduction of inequality, which he in fact achieved through his economic policies and his political activities; Reagan, with the overdog, the person who could still get rich (which is a meaningless concept unless there are others who, by comparison, are relatively poor), so he can be seen as advocating an increase in inequality (which is exactly what he achieved through his economic policies and political activities, such as decreasing taxes on the rich, welfare payments to the poor, the regulation of corporations, and the power of labor unions).

A further contrast between shame ethics and guilt ethics that is relevant to this book is that a central moral commandment of a guilt ethic is "Thou Shalt Not Kill," even when failing to kill makes you vulnerable to being called dishonorable, a coward, a deserter, "soft on crime," etc. A central commandment of a shame ethic is "Thou Shalt Kill," meaning not just that you

---

[2] Franklin D. Roosevelt, "Second Inaugural Address," January 20, 1937 (quoted in Justin Kaplan, gen. ed., *Bartlett's Familiar Quotations*, Boston: Little, Brown, 1992).

[3] Remark at Republican Congressional dinner, Washington, DC, May 4, 1982 (quoted in Kaplan, gen. ed., *Bartlett's Familiar Quotations*, p. 730).

are permitted to kill, but that you are even obligated to, when honor is at stake – which it usually is, for the shame-driven personality. For example, shame ethics supports capital punishment, war, violent self-defense and retaliation, feuds, duels, lynching, torture, and other forms of violence, including "honor killings" – and it defends all of them on moral grounds. In other words, shame ethics and guilt ethics are the same value system except with the value signs reversed, so that what is positively valued by the one is valued negatively by the other.

Among the many thinkers in the past, from the time of the very beginnings of ethical reflection in Western history, who have noticed that there is not just one morality but two and they are opposites, we can include Plato, Aristotle, St. Augustine, and in more recent times, Nietzsche, Thorstein Veblen, and Jean Piaget. Perhaps the most famous such dichotomization of moral value systems is Nietzsche's distinction between "master morality" and "slave morality,"[4] which corresponds very closely to the distinction I am making here between shame ethics and guilt ethics. "Master morality" is the moral value system that justifies being a "master," i.e., a slave-owner (as in the Old South, in the US), and violence in general (e.g., warfare, revenge, sadism). "Slave morality," which Nietzsche identified with Christian ethics as proclaimed by Jesus in his Sermon on the Mount, is the ethic that Nietzsche said would subject

---

[4] See Friedrich Nietzsche, "Beyond Good and Evil" and "The Genealogy of Morals," from *Basic Writings of Nietzsche*, translated, edited, and with an Introduction and notes by Walter Kaufmann, New York: Random House, 2000.

people to becoming or remaining slaves, since it forbids violence even for purposes of self-defense, and recommends that people "turn the other cheek," "resist not evil," forgive those who have hurt them, and love their enemies.

Silvan Tomkins,[5] one of the greatest psychologists of shame in the twentieth century, declared that shame was the dominant motive or dominant emotion motivating right-wing political values and ideologies, and that guilt was the primary motivating force behind left-wing politics. In the contemporary American political climate, left-wing policies, with their emphasis on social and economic equality and providing universal health care, are perceived by many of those who identify with right-wing politics, i.e., the Republican party, as "socialism," if not communism and totalitarianism, whereas the social policies of the right wing are perceived by members of the left wing, the Democrats, as heartless and cruel, even fascism. It is not surprising that those on the left are sometimes called, by their right-wing opponents, not just liberals but "bleeding heart" liberals – for "bleeding heart" is an ancient iconographic symbol for Jesus, whose ethical principles correspond, as Nietzsche saw, to slave-morality or what I am calling guilt-ethics.

Plato and Aristotle distinguish between democracy, an egalitarian political system based on the principle of

---

[5] See Silvan S. Tomkins, "The Right and the Left: A Basic Dimension of Ideology and Personality," pp. 389–411 in R. W. White, ed., *The Study of Lives*, New York: Atherton Press, 1963; and "Ideology and Affect," pp. 109–67 in E. Virginia Demos, ed., *Exploring Affect: The Selected Writings of Silvan S. Tomkins*, Studies in Emotion and Social Interaction, Cambridge: Cambridge University Press, 1995.

rule by the people, and timocracy, whose literal meaning is rule by the honorable (*time*, honor, and *kratia*, rule). The actual, practical meaning of this term, for Plato, was a state governed on principles of honor and military glory (two principles that in historical practice have often been virtually synonymous or indistinguishable, as seen in the fact that throughout history and in cultures around the world aristocrats have most often constituted the military class). To Aristotle it meant a state in which civic honor, i.e., political power, was proportional to one's ownership of property, i.e., one's wealth; i.e., it was rule by the rich, and corresponds to what in today's English adaptations of Greek roots we more commonly call "plutocracy." The latter is a reasonable description of the political system favored by the current conservative Republican majority in the US Supreme Court, with its renunciation of limits on political campaign contributions by the wealthiest individuals and corporations.

Time or honor is the highest value in a shame ethic and in a shame-dominated political culture, and it is often closely associated, and more or less synonymous, with wealth and power. The current US debates over tax policy and many other social and economic debates reflect these distinctions. But they go back to the very beginnings of American democracy, in which the right to vote was originally restricted to those who owned property, or, in other words, capital (i.e., capitalists), as well as to the very beginnings of political thought and practice in Western civilization.

Shame and honor cultures vs. guilt cultures

Anthropologists have made a distinction between shame cultures and guilt cultures, although, in more recent times, the former have more frequently been referred to as honor cultures, or honor and shame cultures. Not all shame cultures are the same, however. Some, recognizing how much destruction and violence can be provoked by shaming people, have institutionalized elaborate rules of courtesy – deep bowing, etc. – which involve humbling oneself so as to avoid shaming anyone else (as in Japan, which, since the end of the Second World War, has come to have both the least economic inequality and the lowest homicide rates in the world). Other, more violent shame cultures specialize in shaming some people in the population as a way of enabling those at the top of the social hierarchy to feel pride and superiority. These are cultures associated with high levels of violence, as I will go into in more detail in the next chapter.

While many different cultures throughout the world have been identified as shame cultures, guilt cultures appear to be extremely rare. Certainly the United States cannot be so described (though it might be called a mixed shame- and guilt-culture, like many others around the world). The clearest example of a relatively pure and extreme guilt culture that I'm aware of is the Hutterites, a very religious, pacifist Anabaptist sect that believes in living according to the precepts of the New Testament. They "consider themselves to . . . live the only true form of Christianity, one which entails communal sharing of property and cooperative production and distribution of goods," as Kaplan and Plaut[6] described them. That is, they conform to the pattern of the earliest Christian communities, as described in the Acts of the Apostles (2:44–5): "all that believed were together, and had all things in common; And sold their possessions and goods, and parted them to all men, as every man had need." In other words, they live according to the principle "from each according to his ability, to each according to his need." As a result, the Hutterites experienced "virtually no differentiation of class, income, or standard of living.... This society comes as close to being classless as any we know."[7] This has been called "primitive (meaning the first or earliest – 'prime' means 'one' – not undeveloped or retarded) Christian communism."[8]

They have lived in communal farms in southern Canada and the north-midwestern United States for more than a century, since emigrating from Eastern Europe to escape religious persecution around 1874. As strict pacifists, that was their only alternative to extermination. Thus, they have no history of collective violence (warfare). An intensive review by medical and social scientists of their well-documented behavioral history and vital statistics during the first 80 years since their arrival in North America reported that "We did not find a single case of murder, assault or rape. Physical aggressiveness of any sort was quite

---

[6] Kaplan and Plaut, *Personality in a Communal Society*.
[7] Ibid., pp. 50 and 30.
[8] P. Miranda, *Communism in the Bible*, Maryknoll, N.Y.: Orbis Books, 1982.

rare."[9] Hostetler,[10] writing 28 years later, reported that there still had not been a single homicide in Hutterite history, throughout the 109 years since the Hutterites immigrated to North America, and only 1 suicide (in a total population that was by then between 40,000 and 50,000). By comparison, if their lethal violence rate had paralleled that of the US as a whole (20 per 100,000 in 1983), they would have experienced 8 to 10 violent deaths in 1983 alone, and 160 to 200 over the 20 years following that, meaning roughly 67–85 homicides and 93–115 suicides – as compared with zero homicides and 1 suicide.

The fact that these estimates are so rough should not blind us to the relevant point, which is that violence can be almost completely prevented. And given how costly violence is in the United States (not to mention the rest of the world), one has to wonder what we value so much more highly than life that we are willing to continue a set of cultural, economic, and political practices that exact such a high cost in death and suffering.

The downside of this culture, for many of the more hedonistic among us, is the high incidence of guilt feelings, which is hardly surprising given the emphasis in this culture on examining oneself scrupulously for any form of sin or violation of their very strict ethical commandments, and their emphasis on blaming themselves rather than others for any problems they experience. Despite that, however, it appears that suicide is almost as non-existent in this culture as homicide – but then, so

[9] Eaton and Weil, *Culture and Mental Disorders.*
[10] John A. Hostetler, *Hutterite Life*, Scottdale, PA: Herald Press, 1983.

are unemployment, homelessness, relative poverty, economic inequality, and the many other causes of lethal violence in the dominant culture of the US. If the emotional costs of this culture include a high frequency and intensity of guilt feelings, the benefits include an almost complete absence of lethal violence. The question I am raising is not whether we must become Hutterites. I take it for granted that that is not a realistic option, but I also do not think it is a necessary one. The question I want to ask is: can we learn something from the Hutterites as to how we might transform our own very different culture into a much less violent one?

The most extreme example of a pure and extreme shame culture in modern Western European history was Nazi Germany (and in modern East Asian history, Germany's ally Japan, before and during the Second World War). Hitler, after all, came to power on the campaign promise to "undo the shame of Versailles," that is, the loss of national honor to which he felt the entire German nation had been subjected by the "war guilt" clause in the Treaty of Versailles and the financial reparations that the Allied Powers demanded Germany pay them; and he made it clear that the only way to undo the shame and regain national honor was by means of virtually unlimited violence. Another more recent political example of the link between shame and violence was the first public statement that Osama bin Laden made after 9/11/2001, when he said that the violence that occurred on that day was a way of making the West taste what he called the "eighty years of humiliation and contempt" to which the entire Islamic nation had been subjected by Europe and America. Again, in the shame ethic that provides the value system for a shame-driven personality in a shame culture, shame can only be wiped out by means of violence, and therefore violence is justified and may even be morally obligated when one has been dishonored.

Shame-driven vs. guilt-ridden personalities

People whose lives and personalities are shaped around shame ethics or guilt ethics can be described as having shame-driven or guilt-ridden characters, respectively. Examples of shame-driven characters would include authoritarian personalities and people whose character structure falls within the borderline or narcissistic spectra of personality types, including anti-social (or criminal) and paranoid personalities. Guilt-ridden personalities would include groups that Freud described as "moral masochists" and "those wrecked by success." Most of us, I think, fall somewhere in between those two extremes.

Shame-driven characters are more likely to commit homicides than guilt-ridden characters, although they may also be prone to suicide as well when that is seen as the only way to escape from overwhelming shame. Guilt-ridden characters, on the other hand, with their abhorrence of violence, are much less likely to commit homicide. They may also be less likely to commit suicide than the shame-driven are, although, when they do commit any lethal violence, it is much more likely to be suicide than homicide.

The shame of it all then stems from the observation

that a shame-driven political value system will engender a party concerned with competition for superior status in an honor–shame hierarchy, a party that will move society in the direction of becoming a more hierarchical, unequal shame culture, which is a recipe for violence. A more egalitarian political ideology shields people from shame by diminishing status differences, so that there is no such thing as being either at the bottom or the top of the totem pole because there is no totem pole. If you go out of your way to make sure that people are not going to be exposed to shame or dishonor or degradation or being forced into a low social caste or class, you will lower the level of violence. The history of violence in America during the twentieth century under the two different political parties appears to bear this out.

5

Who Wants To Be
Redundant?

In Britain, the unemployed are referred to as "redundant" – which, of course, they are from the standpoint of the employer and the economy. But human beings cannot survive psychologically when they experience themselves as being redundant: unnecessary, unneeded, of no worth or value to any company or employer. It can be very difficult, and for some people impossible, to maintain a sense of self-esteem or self-respect when one is being treated as worthless by a part of the world that we all need in order to remain psychologically healthy: the world of work. The loss of a job is, of course, only one among the several determinants that must be present in order to cause behavior as destructive and costly as homicide or suicide. But when the other determinants are already in place, becoming unemployed can become the last straw that overwhelms a person's shaky defenses against collapse – just as remaining employed may provide just (barely) enough support to neutralize whatever other assaults on self-esteem and self-respect a person is experiencing.

The inextricable relationship between unemployment and shame runs through all the research and writing on the subject, for few experiences in life can cause people to feel so overwhelmingly humiliated and rejected. Thomas Cottle[1] titled one chapter of his book on the psychological effects of being laid-off from one's job "The Shame of Unemployment," and one reader wrote:

> I purchased this title as part of an effort to understand what happened to my family when my father was fired and was subsequently unable to replace his job. The book was almost unbearably sad to read, but it rang absolutely true to the way I remember this crisis and its effects on my father and our family, *especially the overwhelming sense of shame we all lived with* ... [the long-term unemployed] aren't lazy, useless folks to be disposed of but *human beings with souls who have experienced what amounts to a life tragedy.*[2]

As these comments indicate, unemployment does not affect just the person who has lost a job; it also has profound direct and indirect effects on the person's family and community. To shift to another level of analysis, a high unemployment rate not only harms the unemployed, it also harms those who still do have jobs, both objectively and subjectively in that a high unemployment rate drives down wages and increases insecurity, which is in itself painful but also a barrier to effective bargaining for better wages and working conditions.

---

[1] Thomas Cottle, *Hardest Times: The Trauma of Long-Term Unemployment*, Amherst: University of Massachusetts Press, 2001.
[2] L. Major, retrieved from Amazon.com: customer review of ibid., emphasis added.

The "ripple effects" of unemployment thus ultimately damage everyone except, perhaps, employers, who can reduce their labor costs and neglect worker safety, though even they may suffer in the long run if poverty becomes so widespread that their potential customers can no longer afford to buy their products or services.

That is why the individuals who react to increases in the rate or duration of unemployment with homicide or suicide (or both) may not be limited to those who are themselves unemployed. Entire groups of those who are already most socially and economically vulnerable even before the unemployment rate increases can hardly avoid the stresses and frustrations caused by "job insecurity," the palpable and multiple changes that occur in relations between companies and workers, for everyone who lives from paycheck to paycheck, when unemployment increases: lower wages; fewer job opportunities; less bargaining power; fewer grievance procedures; less assurance that one will not lose one's only source of income in the near future, no matter how hard one works; having more and more unemployed relatives and friends who need one's help (and fewer who could be of help to oneself in an emergency), and so on. When these multiple stresses become overwhelming, when added to whatever other stresses people are already experiencing, we should not be surprised when an increasing number of the most psychologically and economically vulnerable individuals, whether they are themselves unemployed or not, attempt to relieve the pressure by resorting to violence of one type or another (suicide, homicide, or both).

Another scholar, Katherine Newman,[3] also draws our attention to the centrality of shame. Writing about the desperation with which ghetto residents avoid the shame of unemployment by working at humiliating poverty-level jobs, she titles her book *No Shame in My Game*. To illustrate her point, she quotes a young woman who "has had to confront the degradation that comes from holding a 'low job'" at a fast-food outlet, but since "her dignity is underwritten by the critique she has absorbed about the 'welfare-dependent,'" she says, "I'm not ashamed because I have a job" – meaning she would be ashamed if she did not have one, even a humiliating one. "Most people don't" have a job (which is actually true in the neighborhood in which she lives), "and I'm proud of myself that . . . I'm not on welfare" (p. 98) – which, of course, implies that she would be ashamed if she had to be on welfare.

Newman identifies the underlying dynamic of shame vs. honor when she reflects on

> why exclusion from the society of the employed is such a devastating source of social isolation. We could hand people money . . . but we can't hand out honor. Honor comes from participation in this central setting in our culture and from the positive identity it confers. Roosevelt understood this during the Great Depression and responded with the creation of thousands of publicly funded jobs designed to put people to work building the national parks, the railway stations . . . Social scientists studying the unemployed in the 1930s showed that

---

[3] Katherine Newman, *No Shame in My Game: The Working Poor in the Inner City*, New York: Vintage Books and Russell Sage Foundation, 1999.

people who held WPA [Works Progress Administration] jobs were far happier and healthier than those who were on the dole, even when their incomes did not differ significantly. WPA workers had their dignity in the midst of poverty; those on the dole were vilified and could not justify their existence. (p. 104)

All of this is consistent with our analysis of shame. Newman sums up the psychological necessity of work for emotional survival and the devastating effect of being without it:

Given our tradition of equating moral value with employment, it stands to reason that the most profound dividing line in our culture is that separating the working person from the unemployed. Only after this canyon has been crossed do we begin to make the finer gradations that distinguish white-collar worker from blue-collar worker, CEO from secretary . . . We inhabit an unforgiving culture that is blind to the many reasons why some people cross that employment barrier and others are left behind. While we may remember, for a time, that unemployment rates are high, . . . in the end American culture wipes these background truths out in favor of a simpler dichotomy: the worthy and the unworthy, the working stiff and the lazy sloth. . . . In the United States, . . . those outside the employment system are categorized as unworthy and made to feel it. (p. 87)

In short, to be unemployed is to be shamed.

The word "redundant" is not applied to old people, but it is a feeling that old people often struggle with. When Roosevelt proposed the social security plan and succeeded in getting it through Congress, he was speaking to these concerns. The elderly, who had previously had the highest poverty rate of any age group, were to be shielded from abandonment. Since the elderly have the highest suicide rate of any age group, policies that protect the elderly from feeling redundant (forgotten, abandoned, useless) should result in lower suicide rates. This is what happened under Roosevelt and through the New Deal Era. It is noteworthy that some contemporary Republicans are now trying to abolish social security, along with the rest of the New Deal and even earlier progressive reforms going back to Woodrow Wilson and the changes that have occurred in the political and economic institutions of the US since early in the twentieth century, such as income taxes and new regulatory agencies.

6

Red States, Blue States: Honor vs. Guilt

On the morning of November 8, 2000, Americans woke up to see a startling map on their television screens and in their newspapers. The country was divided politically by region and regional culture into "Red States" and "Blue States." In this disputed election, the Red States were those that voted for the Republican, Bush, and the Blue States for the Democrat, Gore. Although it was not immediately apparent, it eventually became clear that this division was not merely political. It was also a division between more violent and less violent cultures within the US.

When we compare the Red States with the Blue, we find that the Republican-dominated states had significantly higher rates of homicide (both legal and illegal) and suicide than the Democratic-majority states, both in 2000 and 2004.[1] At first blush, this may seem

---

[1] In 2000, 30 states were Red and 20 were Blue, and in 2004, 31 states were Red and 19 Blue, though the total populations of the two groups of states were almost identical, since the Blue States, being more urban, had larger populations per state. Between the two elections, only 3 of the 50 states

surprising, given that one would assume that both sets of states include sizeable minorities of members of the losing party. In fact, however, of the 31 Red States in 2004, fully half had 50 percent more Bush voters than Kerry supporters (i.e., the vote margin in Bush's favor was 60/40). The Blue States were much more evenly divided with only 2 of 19 showing that degree of polarization. Looked at another way, the Pew Research Center's post-election "political typology"[2] pointed out that while Bush's margin of victory, 2.4 percent, was the smallest of any victorious incumbent in US history, "in most of the country, the 2004 race wasn't even close to being close ... In the majority of the nation's 3,153 counties, the election was a landslide – with either Mr. Bush or Mr. Kerry winning by a margin of at least twenty percentage points." Many observers of the Red State / Blue State divide have pointed out that there is an increasing tendency throughout the country for people with similar political values and allegiances to congregate together in the same neighborhoods, sub-urbs, or regions, thus adding to political polarization and reinforcing the differences between partisans of the two parties.

Up to now, I have been examining differences that occur over time (1900–2007) within the same popula-

in the US switched sides: New Hampshire, which had been Red in 2000, became Blue in 2004; and Iowa and New Mexico, which had been Blue in 2000, became Red in 2004.

[2] The Pew Research Center for the People and the Press, "The 2005 Political Typology: Beyond Red vs. Blue: Republicans Divided about Role of Government – Democrats by Social and Personal Values," May 10, 2005. Downloaded from www.people-press.org on 8/30/2007.

tion, that of the US. Now, I want to look at differences between different populations – those of the Red States versus those of the Blue States – that exist at the same time: the year 2000, and again in the year 2004.

Regardless of which way of looking at the relationship between political parties and violence I use, I find the same result: more violence in Republican-dominated *regions* just as there was in Republican-dominated *eras*, and less violence in the regions as well as the eras of Democratic hegemony. However, these two ways of looking at the correlation between party and violence are not identical in every respect. For example, unemployment rates were not significantly different in the Red States from what they were in the Blue States in either 2000 or 2004. Rather, the difference between Red and Blue States seems to reflect a difference in culture and in the voters themselves.

The Red State / Blue State polarization can remind us that the causal arrow runs in both directions: the correlations between Republican majorities in the electorate and higher rates of lethal violence and between Democratic majorities and decreases in violence, may not be due simply to the effects of Republican and Democratic policies on the population. They may also be a result of preexisting attitudes and values of the different population groups that led them to vote for Republicans or Democrats in the first place. It is not merely that the parties' policies affect and influence citizens' feelings and behavior; it is also true that citizens' attitudes and values shape and influence the parties, not least in the sense that it is their values and attitudes that determine whether or not a given party will win an election and come to power. So, by the time either of the two parties triumphs, the voters who elected them may already be primed with the same values and attitudes as the party they voted for. It is true that much research has shown that the leaders of the two parties are, on average, more politically polarized than the voters are. But that does not negate another finding, which is that there are major differences between the regional cultures of the Red States and the Blue, and between Republican and Democratic voters.

Among the many lines of evidence supporting this difference in political culture and personality are studies of the contrasting practices, values, and attitudes concerning guns, militarism, torture, capital punishment, imprisonment, corporal punishment of children and other indices of violence, force, and coercion that differentiated Red States from Blue, and Republican voters from Democratic ones, in the 2000 and 2004 presidential elections. For example, the Pew Research Center interviewed 2,000 adults in the month after the 2004 election and were able to differentiate Republican vs. Democratic voters on a number of dimensions that clearly involve values and attitudes concerning the use of force and violence. On the basis of this, they developed a "political typology" that identified numerous areas in which Republican voters were far more likely than Democratic ones to see the use of violence as both an effective and an acceptable means of resolving social problems and conflicts. For example, they report that "for the most part, *opinions about the use of force are what divides Democratic-oriented groups from the*

Republican groups" (emphasis added).[3] This difference appeared in every aspect of life, from personal to political.

The Pew political typology divided voters into several groups based on their social, political, economic, and moral values. The groups whose members were most likely to have voted for Bush were those they called "Enterprisers" and "Social Conservatives." They found that gun ownership was much more prevalent among Republican groups, especially Enterprisers and Social Conservatives, than among Democrats. Solid majorities (56–59 percent) in both of those Republican-oriented groups say they have guns in their home as opposed to 23 percent of the most strongly Democratic group, which Pew calls "Liberals," and barely more among other Democratic sub-groups. This carries over into attitudes toward the National Rifle Association, toward which 80 percent of the Social Conservatives or Enterprisers have a favorable opinion, as opposed to 20 percent of the most solidly Democratic group, the Liberals.

These attitudes also extend to their views of foreign and military policy, so that "foreign affairs assertiveness now almost completely distinguishes Republican-oriented voters from Democratic-oriented voters." At the same time, "beyond their staunch opposition to the war in Iraq, Democrats overwhelmingly believe that effective diplomacy, rather than military strength, should serve as the basis for US security policy." For example, 70 percent of Enterprisers but

---

[3] Ibid., p. 7.

only 8 percent of Liberals believe that "the best way to ensure peace is through military strength," whereas 88 percent of Liberals and only 13 percent of Enterprisers believe that "good diplomacy is the best way to ensure peace." Pew found that 90 percent of Liberals, but only 9 percent of Enterprisers, believe that "relying too much on force creates hatred and more terrorism," whereas 84 percent of Enterprisers believe that "military force is the best way to defeat terrorism," as compared with only 7 percent of Liberals.

> In fact, public values about ... the use of military force are among the *only* value dimensions in which Republican and Democratic groups clearly align on opposite sides. ... The extreme partisan polarization over the war in Iraq in recent years is interwoven with sharply divided judgments about ... assertiveness. Asked whether the best way to ensure peace is through military strength or through good diplomacy, the vast majority in all three Democratic-leaning groups choose diplomacy, while those in Republican-leaning groups express more confidence in military strength. While the degree of intensity within partisan groups may differ, there is a significantly greater difference of opinion between parties than there is within either party coalition. This partisan divide is even broader when it comes to people's views on the war on terrorism. Across all Republican groups, most believe that using overwhelming military force is the best way to defeat terrorism around the world, while a clear majority in all Democratic groups believe relying too much on military force to defeat terrorism creates hatred that leads to more terrorism.[4]

---

[4] Ibid., p. 22.

"On many national security issues, especially the war in Iraq, internal partisan fissures," – meaning differences within each party – "are overshadowed by the vast gulf dividing Republicans and Democrats." Nearly 90 percent of Enterprisers believe the pre-emptive use of military force is "often or sometimes" justified, and only 10 percent (as compared with two-thirds of Liberals) believe it is "rarely or never" justified. In general, then, "Support for the use of military force is strongest among groups that are reliably Republican, somewhat less so among centrist groups, and weakest among Democratic groups." When asked whether torture of suspected terrorists can be justified, Enterprisers were three times as likely as Liberals (63 percent vs. 21 percent) to say that it "often or sometimes" can, whereas a solid 77 percent of Liberals said that it "rarely or never" could be justified.

Patterns of violence in Red States and Blue States

So far, I have differentiated Republican from Democratic voters on the basis of their different attitudes toward different forms of violence. But the Red and Blue States also differ in their rates of lethally violent behavior, i.e., suicide and homicide, including the legal form of the latter, capital punishment (the death penalty). With respect to the suicide rate, in 2000 the Red States had a rate of 13 per 100,000 and the Blue States only 10. In 2004, the suicide rate in Red States was 13.9 vs. the Blue States' 10.2. Homicide rates in the Red States were 5.7 in both 2000 and 2004 whereas in the Blue States they were 4.2 and 4.0 in those years. The difference between Red and Blue States in total lethal violence rates (suicide plus homicide) in 2000 was 18.7 vs. 14.2 and in 2004, 19.6 vs. 14.2. The probability that differences of these magnitudes in both of these years were due to chance was less than 1 in 10,000. The capital punishment rate differences are even more startling. Between 1976 (when capital punishment was reinstituted in the US after having been declared unconstitutional in 1972) and 2009, the Red States executed 1,177 people and the Blues States 54: a ratio of more than 20 to1. Of the 14 states with the most executions, every one is a Red State (11 of them Southern states). Of the 14 states with no death penalty, 10 are Blue States. Of the 31 Red States in 2004, 27 have a death penalty.

The significance of this is not only in the deaths of all of the individuals who were killed over those 33 years, but also in what they communicate to the rest of us as a matter of cultural and moral symbolism. The figures on capital punishment tell us that, at the highest and most authoritative levels of the legal and governmental system in the Red States, there is official, public approval of the principle that killing people, or in other words committing homicide (meaning the killing of another human being by a human being), is an effective and morally and legally acceptable way of expressing disapproval of another person, punishing him (because it almost always is him), and achieving justice. What effect does this have on rates of homicide and suicide in the public at large in these states? The late Justice Louis Brandeis wrote in 1928 that "Our government is the potent, the omnipresent teacher. For good or ill, it teaches the whole people by its example." Brandeis went on to explain why it was so important that government officials not break the law, but, where he spoke of crime, I would speak of violence. He said "Crime is contagious. If the government becomes a lawbreaker, it breeds contempt for laws; it invites every man to become a law unto himself; it invites anarchy."[5] In other words, to paraphrase his remarks, violence is contagious. If the government commits homicide, it breeds contempt for non-violence; it invites every man to commit homicide for himself; it does indeed invite anarchy, the breakdown of the very "law and order" in whose name capital punishment is most often defended.

These attitudes toward the use of violence then carry over into approval of corporal punishment of children, gun ownership and use, and approaches to foreign and military policy. There are higher rates of gun ownership in the Red States than in the Blue,[6] and, not surprisingly, higher rates of death from guns by all three means by which guns kill people – homicide, suicide, and so-called "accidents."

The incarceration rate is significantly higher in the

---

[5] Quoted in Charles E. Silberman, *Criminal Violence, Criminal Justice*, New York: Random House, 1978, p. 47.

[6] Philip J. Cook and Mark H. Moore report that the highest prevalence of gun ownership is in the states of the Mountain Census Region, followed by the South and Midwest (which is precisely the geographic distribution of the Red States). They also report that "The prevalence of gun ownership differs rather widely across urban areas, from around 10% in the cities of the Northeast [i.e., Blue States] to more than 50% in the Mountain states [Red States]." See their article, "Guns, Gun Control, and Homicide," pp. 246–23 in M. Dwayne Smith and Margaret A. Zahn, eds., *Studying and Preventing Homicide: Issues and Challenges*, Thousand Oaks, CA, London, and New Delhi: SAGE Publications, 1999, pp. 248 and 255.

Red than in the Blue States. In the year 2000, the average incarceration rate in the Red States was 712 per 100,000 as opposed to 487 in the Blue States. If rates of capital punishment and imprisonment can be seen as indices of punitiveness, it is clear that the Red States lead the Blue States or exceed the Blue States with respect to both their rates of violence and their levels of punitiveness.

To understand why these two groups of states differ as they do, it is necessary both to understand the cultural differences between them – to see the extent to which they represent two contrasting cultures – and to understand how these two groups of voters differ as they do. That is, it is necessary to identify their differences in attitudes and values, the dimensions of personality that go to make up what has traditionally been called "character."

With only slight oversimplification, the Red States can be described as consisting mostly of the "Old South" and the "Wild West," meaning the 11 former slave-owning states plus two border states, Kentucky and Oklahoma, and the Western mountain and desert states and most of the Midwestern Great Plains states – the states most associated with the historical heritage and symbolism of "Cowboys and Indians." The Blue States, by contrast, occupy both coasts – the Pacific and Northern Atlantic coasts and New England – as well as the North Central states with a strong Scandinavian heritage, such as Wisconsin and Minnesota, together with Illinois and Michigan.

There is by now a small library of studies by historians, anthropologists, psychologists, and political scientists describing and documenting these differences.[7] One repeated finding is the identification of the American South or the Southern states as a culture whose salient moral values exist along the polarity from shame to honor. Another recurrent finding is that the sensitivity to shame in this culture is a direct cause of the increased degree of violence. These patterns can be traced back into the nineteenth century, as can the contrast with the relatively less violent New England states of the North, in which guilt and conscience were apparently more central products and engenderers of what has been described as relatively more of a "guilt culture" than the South. For example, as Wyatt-Brown has summarized a great deal of historical evidence, "child-rearing practices in the antebellum South subjected the young to ... shame and humiliation and the ideals of hierarchy and honor, a mode in sharp contrast to the conscience-building techniques of pious Yankees."[8]

"Honor" in the southern culture of honor is not simply an abstract "brooding omnipresence in the sky" (as Oliver Wendell Holmes said the common law was not) but, rather, a concrete reality that was codified many times in the history of the South in written documents called "Codes of Honor." These written honor codes

---

[7] See the most complete treatment of these subjects, Bertram Wyatt-Brown, *Southern Honor: Ethics and Behavior in the Old South*, Oxford and New York: Oxford University Press, 1982, and an abridged version of the same, *Honor and Violence in the Old South,* Oxford and New York: Oxford University Press, 1986. See also Richard E. Nisbett and Dov Cohen, *Culture of Honor: The Psychology of Violence in the South*, Boulder, CO, and Oxford: Westview Press, 1996; also Edward L. Ayers, *Vengeance and Justice: Crime and Punishment in the 19th-Century American South*, New York and Oxford: Oxford University Press, 1984.

[8] Wyatt-Brown, *Southern Honor*, p. 118.

consisted of detailed sets of rules as to how men could defend their honor by means of violence such as dueling, and the conditions under which they would have to resort to violence in order to save their honor. The codes of honor can be seen as examples as the codification of shame ethics. Where a guilt culture's central moral code, which I have called a guilt-ethic, counsels people who are struck on one cheek to turn the other, the codes of honor prescribe exactly the opposite behavior: fight a duel. Dueling was not unknown in the North, of course, but it was never as widespread, and died out sooner and more completely than in the South. That is one reason why the South became the dueling center of America, a tradition of acceptance and approval of violence that continues to the present day in other forms, as shown by the statistics on violent death and other types of violence.

Another form of socially recognized and accepted violence that occurred publicly and with regular ritual patterns was the practice of lynching,[9] the very name of which is that of a Southern gentleman. Lynching was not simply a private act; it was well known to and condoned by the legal authorities, thus exemplifying the acceptance of violence by the community, including its political leaders. While lynching is now outlawed and dueling has become archaic, the use of violence to settle personal disputes and express moral disapproval of other people continues in the South of today, as indicated by the high murder rates and the disproportionate use of capital punishment.

[9] See Orlando Patterson, *Rituals of Blood: Consequences of Slavery in Two American Centuries*, New York: Basic Books, 1998.

The codes of honor can be seen as the codification of shame ethics, and the interaction between shame and politics in the Southern states can be illustrated by Lyndon Johnson's remark concerning the "Bourbon strategy" that I referred to previously. He said that it was to the political and economic advantage of the Bourbons (the white ruling class) that racial discrimination continue in the South, because, as long as it did, the poor whites would have an even poorer group of blacks whom they could look down upon and to whom they could feel superior.

Indeed, the historical precursor of present-day racial discrimination in the South, slavery, has also been described in much the same terms[10] as a means by which slave-ownership was seen as a source of honor for the masters, a sign of their superiority to an inferior caste (the black slaves) and also to non-slave-owning whites (who were called a variety of demeaning names, from "crackers" and "red necks" – referring to the sunburn they got from working in the fields – to "white trash").

Even when shame and its opposite, honor – rather than guilt vs. innocence – are the central moral emotions and the central forms of moral blame and praise in a society, which is how the term "shame culture" was originally defined by Ruth Benedict,[11] different societies that can be described as belonging to that general

---

[10] See Orlando Patterson, *Slavery and Social Death: A Comparative Study*, Cambridge, MA: Harvard University Press, 1982; and Kenneth S. Greenberg, *Honor and Slavery*, Princeton: Princeton University Press, 1996.

[11] Ruth Benedict, *The Chrysanthemum and the Sword: Patterns of Japanese Culture* (1946), Rutland, VT, and Tokyo: Charles E. Tuttle, 1970.

category can vary enormously with respect to how frequently and severely they subject their members to experiences of being shamed and humiliated, and how successfully they provide those who have been shamed with non-violent means of redeeming their honor. As I mentioned above, on p. 111, some societies, which we might call "mild" shame cultures, such as contemporary (post-World War II) Japan, recognizing how much destruction and violence can be stimulated by shame (and had been, in their not-so-distant past), have evolved codes of etiquette designed to protect people from even inadvertent or unintentional shaming. Other societies, such as the American South, which can be called more "extreme" shame cultures, may also expect people to obey strict rules of etiquette as a way to avoid treating others or being treated by others with disrespect; but they nevertheless have retained some practices that, in both the past and the present, have functioned as recipes for stimulating the emotion of shame and the behavior of violence. One of these is a high degree of social stratification (whether by class, caste, race, gender, age, religion, ethnicity, or any other means by which people are divided into the superior and the inferior). Slavery was perhaps the most extreme version of this, but stratification by race continues by other means in the present,[12] such as the disproportionate imprisonment and disenfranchisement to which African-Americans have been subjected. To condemn some sub-groups in

---

[12] See Alexander, *The New Jim Crow*; also Robert Perkinson, *Texas Tough: The Rise of America's Prison Empire,* New York: Metropolitan Books, Henry Holt and Company, 2010.

the population to a lower place in the status hierarchy is to subject them to feelings of shame and humiliation, for they are treated with contempt as inferior beings. It is thus only to be expected that a higher level of violence would result, as it does in the South.

I have focused on the South because it is clearly the core strategic region that has been most responsible for the resurgence of the Republican party to power, beginning in 1966–8 and continuing in most of the years since then. Since the success of the Republicans' "southern strategy" in 1966 and 1968, the Republican party has consistently received a majority of white votes and has succeeded in blocking virtually all further civil rights legislation; and the Southern states, having become almost completely Republican in their political allegiances, have become the determining factor in Republican electoral victories.

The history, the cultural heritage, and symbolism of the "Wild West" is as well known and palpable as the honor culture of the Old South. As in the South, male honor was dependent, to a much greater degree than in the more established and peaceful culture of New England and the Eastern seaboard, on men's ability and willingness to demonstrate both their courage and their expertise in the arts of violence. Students of honor, such as the British anthropologist Julian Pitt-Rivers,[13] have commented that disputes of honor can only be settled

---

[13] Julian Pitt-Rivers, "Honor and Social Status," pp. 19–77 in J. G. Peristiany, ed., *Honour and Shame: The Values of Mediterranean Society*, Chicago: University of Chicago Press, 1966, pp. 30–1; Julian Pitt-Rivers, "Honor," pp. 503–11 in *International Encyclopedia of the Social Sciences*, 1968, pp. 509–10.

outside the law, between the persons involved. While that is a characteristic of honor cultures in general, as in the extra-legal patterns of violence in the South (duels, feuds, lynching parties), the relative absence of effective law and government in much of the history of the Western states only exacerbated and reinforced and legitimized this tradition. The cultural heritage left by the history of the Wild West is one in which personal honor can be maintained only by personal violence outside the law. Another related similarity between the Old South and the Wild West is that this cultural pattern is dependent on, and predicated on, the private ownership of guns. Thus, it is not surprising that the areas of the US in which guns are most widely valued, owned, and used, and in which the death rates from guns are at their highest, are the Southern and Western states.

Shame cultures have a universal tendency to create not just a class system but also a caste system, meaning a status system of much greater rigidity and impermeability, thus allowing for much less social mobility than a class system. A member of a lower caste can never escape his place in the caste hierarchy, no matter how successful he or she is in other respects. The lowest caste in the Southern shame culture was the African-Americans; in the West, it was the Native Americans. Today the fight in the US over immigration, especially that of Mexican Americans, is the arena in which many of these shame-culture status contests are being fought out. The issue, however, is always the same: namely, how can those who have a need to feel pride, because that is the only alternative to feelings of shame, maintain their pride and avoid shame except by casting some groups in the population as inferiors whom they can therefore look down upon and to whom they can feel superior: the "Bourbon strategy" writ large. Unfortunately, this is also a recipe for violence.

There is always a reciprocity between culture and personality in the sense that different types of cultures produce different types of personalities through their child-rearing, socialization, and educational practices and the conventions of their criminal justice systems, their religious beliefs and practices, and other social institutions, and those personalities in turn reproduce the culture. Shame cultures typically produce shame-driven personalities and guilt cultures typically produce guilt-ridden personalities (hence such phrases as "guilty white liberal" and "bleeding-heart liberal"). Both of these personality types and differences have been studied mostly in terms of their psychopathology, with "borderline," narcissistic, paranoid, anti-social, and "right-wing authoritarian" character structures seen as characteristic of shame-driven people, and "moral masochists," as well as depressive and obsessional personality patterns, seen as more typical of guilt-ridden personalities. For the purposes of this book, however, the relationship between personality and political attitudes is more relevant. This has been the focus of much research in recent decades contrasting authoritarian with egalitarian personalities.[14]

---

[14] The distinctions originally made between shame and guilt cultures by Ruth Benedict (*The Chrysanthemum and the Sword*), and between authoritarian and egalitarian personalities (Theodor W. Adorno, E. Frenkel-Brunswick, D. J. Levinson, and R. N. Sanford, *The Authoritarian Personality*, New York: Harper and Row, 1950), were both called into

The usefulness of these distinctions in the present context stems in part from their explanatory value with respect to figure 1.1 showing the correlation between the two political parties and the contrasting patterns of lethal violence associated with each. The contrast between shame and guilt cultures corresponds in most respects to the contrasts between the Red States and the Blue States as well as the contrasts between the social and economic policies of the Republican and Democratic parties. In tying these contrasts to the

question by critics soon after they were first formulated. One result of that is that these concepts have been refined and are now once again very much in use. There is an extensive and quite sophisticated anthropological litera-ture on cultures of shame and honor in the circum-Mediterranean culture area and the Arab world, as well as in Japan and the American South. See also Pitt-Rivers, "Honor"; Pitt-Rivers, "Honor and Social Status"; J. G. Peristiany and Julian Pitt-Rivers, eds., "Introduction," in *Honor and Grace in Anthropology*, Cambridge: Cambridge University Press, 1992; Peristiany, *Honour and Shame*; Edwin O. Reischauer, *The United States and Japan*, 3rd edn., Cambridge, MA: Harvard University Press, 1965; David D. Gilmore, ed., *Honor and Shame and the Unity of the Mediterranean*, Washington, DC: American Anthropological Association, 1987.

See also Michelle Rosaldo, ed., *Towards an Anthropology of the Emotions: Rethinking Shame and Guilt* (Proceedings of a Symposium of the American Anthropological Association), Washington, DC: American Anthropological Association, 1983. As Rosaldo wrote in this volume, "of all themes in the literature on culture and personality the opposition between guilt and shame has probably proven most resilient" (p. 135).

In the psychological literature, there is also a renewed recognition of the usefulness of an old concept, "right-wing authoritarianism," in part through the work of Robert Altemeyer. See especially his book *The Authoritarian Specter*, Cambridge, MA, and London: Harvard University Press, 1996; also his *Right-Wing Authoritarianism*, Winnipeg: University of Manitoba Press, 1981; and his *Enemies of Freedom: Understanding Right-Wing Authoritarianism*, San Francisco: Jossey-Bass, 1988.

And see Marc J. Hetherington and Jonathan D. Weiler, *Authoritarianism and Polarization in American Politics*, Cambridge: Cambridge University Press, 2009.

data on high and low rates of homicide and suicide, it becomes necessary to consider the differences between people who vote Republican and those who vote for the Democrats, and here the personality distinctions become central. Shame cultures produce shame-driven personalities who are especially vulnerable to suicidal and homicidal behavior when subjected to a degree of humiliation that is greater than they are able to tolerate. But shame-driven personalities reproduce shame cultures, e.g., Republican administrations whose policies tend to create the conditions of inferiority that generate feelings of shame. Thus it is not that Republican voters themselves are necessarily the ones who are committing more acts of homicide or suicide; it is that they are creating a social hierarchy that casts some demographic groups – e.g. African-Americans and in some cases Latinos and Native Americans – into an inferior social status that subjects them to disproportionate amounts of shame and contempt and thereby stimulates increased rates of homicide and/or suicide.

Among whites, suicide rates are highest among white gun-owning males in the Western states, but they are highest of all among Native Americans, many of whom also live in those states. Here again, the culture of shame creates a climate of violence.

Authoritarian personalities have been distinguished from egalitarian personalities with respect to several differences in values and attitudes. For example, authoritarian personalities are more likely to approve of social inequality, hierarchies, and status differences, and to sanction the use of violence by authority figures such as policemen, soldiers, judges, and jailers. They believe not only in dividing people into the opposing categories of superior and inferior, but in regarding their own demographic group as the superior one. Common examples: whites are superior to people of color, the rich are superior to the poor, the old are superior to the young, and men are superior to women. The success of appealing to people by means of such stereotypes can be seen in the fact that, since 1968, Republicans have received a majority of the votes of those who are white, wealthy, older, and male.

As the research on authoritarianism has become more sophisticated in its methodology, one finding has become clearer: namely, that authoritarianism is associated with right-wing political attitudes and values. To speak of right-wing authoritarianism is essentially a redundancy. As Norberto Bobbio, an Italian political scientist, has pointed out in his book *Left and Right,* right-wing political movements place a positive value on social inequality and status hierarchies just as left-wing political ideologies pursue greater social and economic equality. Thus right-wing politics is completely consistent with the value positions of authoritarian personalities. The preference for authoritarian aggression, that is the use of force by government authorities, is reflected in the greater use of capital punishment and imprisonment in the Red States vs. the Blue States. Altemeyer and his colleagues have concluded, from extensive and repeated studies of authoritarian vs. egalitarian attitudes and values over several decades among Republican and Democratic voters and legislators throughout the United States, that there is a remarkably consistent and statistically significant correlation between authoritarianism and membership in the Republican party, and between egalitarian beliefs and Democratic party affiliations, among both voters and legislators. They found a similar correlation between conservative voters and legislators in Canada, who scored high on the "Right-Wing Authoritarianism" (RWA) attitudes and values scale, whereas those affiliated with liberal party politics scored low. Although most of their research in the US was performed before the "Red State / Blue State" distinction was first made, in 2000, what they found reveals some very interesting inter-correlations between all three of these variables: character, party, and state. In eight studies undertaken during the 1990s, they studied the mean scores of state legislators on the RWA scale, by party and state. They found that: (1) all Republicans scored above the mean on the RWA scale, whether they were from Red or Blue States, with the single exception of those from a Blue State, Connecticut – and even their scores were higher than those of any of the Blue State Democrats; (2) Democratic legislators in Blue States all scored below the mean; (3) the only Democratic legislators who scored above the mean were those from Red States. These results would appear to be consistent with the proposition that culture (Red State vs. Blue State), personality (authoritarian vs. egalitarian), and party identification (Republican vs. Democratic) influence and reinforce each other.[15]

---

[15] Robert Altemeyer, *The Authoritarian Specter*, Cambridge, MA, and London: Harvard University Press, 1996, pp. 291–6, and figure 11.2, p. 292.

I can imagine my readers objecting at this point: "Aren't you guilty of doing exactly what you are accusing authoritarian personalities, and by extension Republicans, of doing: namely, dividing the population into a superior in-group vs. an inferior out-group and putting yourself among the superior?" Or, to put it more bluntly, "Aren't you shaming and blaming Republicans, and everyone who lives in a Red State, and thus in effect promoting violence?" My questioner could continue: "Aren't you guilty of doing what those shame-driven people called 'borderline personalities' do, and splitting people into those who are all good (from your point of view, Democrats and Blue States) and those who are all bad (Republicans and Red States), with yourself in the all good camp?"

So let me be as clear as possible about something that up to this point I have felt was too obvious to need to be mentioned: neither the Democrats nor the Blue States are all good, nor do the Republicans and the Red States have any monopoly on evil. For example, even the lowest violence rates achieved under Democrats would be considered epidemics of murder in every other developed nation on earth, and the suicide levels, even at their lowest under Democrats, are still significantly higher than those in many other developed countries of the world.[16] For example, the US in 1998, when it had the lowest lethal violence rates for the past 30 years, still had a rate of 17.3 violent deaths per 100,000 per year, consisting of a homicide rate of 6.9 and a suicide rate

[16] The figures cited here are from Etienne G. Krug, Linda L. Dahlberg, James A. Mercy, Anthony B. Zwi, and Rafael Lozano, *World Report on Violence and Health*, Geneva: World Health Organization, 2002, tables A.8–A.9, pp. 308–21.

of 10.4. Comparing the US with the country that is perhaps closest culturally to it, namely, its mother country, the UK, that country's homicide and suicide rates were 0.8 and 6.8, respectively, in 1999, which means a total lethal violence rate of only 7.6 – a homicide rate only 11 percent of that in the US, a suicide rate some 35 percent lower, and a lethal violence rate only about 40 percent of that in the US.

In fact, during the late 1990s, all 19 of the other largest economically developed countries in the world (consisting of Western Europe, the other English-speaking democracies, and Japan) had an average lethal violence rate of 12.7, as compared with the US rate of 17.3. The US murder rate, at 6.9, was more than 6 times as high as the average rate of 1.1 in the other 19 countries. Only their suicide rates (11.5) were close to those of the US (10.4), and the US suicide rate itself had also been 11.5 as recently as 1991, before Clinton became president, and much higher than that (13.3) in 1975.

As for the Red State / Blue State distinction, I lived in one of the bluest of the Blue States, Massachusetts, from 1966, when the white backlash against the civil rights revolution became the national movement that brought the Republicans back into power throughout the US, and found that even that Blue State had enough capacity for overt racial discrimination to put to rest any assumption that Red States had a monopoly on that particular form of authoritarian ethnocentrism.[17]

---

[17] For a prize-winning account of the racial conflicts that occurred in Boston during this era, see J. Anthony Lukas, *Common Ground: A Turbulent Decade in the Lives of Three American Families*, New York: Knopf, 1985.

So let me emphasize that medicine is not in the business of making value judgments except about one thing which is its *raison d'être*, and that is the value – the sanctity, if you will – of human life (and by extension, of other life as well, both for its own sake and because human life is absolutely dependent on the continued existence of other living things – the more different species, the better). The issue I am addressing in this book is lethal violence, the rates of which can be taken as a measure of the psychological, social, and political health of a nation. My job as a physician is to diagnose ill health, to discover its causes, and to prescribe remedies that will cure illness and promote healing. To get involved in blaming or shaming is not such a remedy, but recognizing and publicizing relevant facts are, I hope, even if the facts may at first seem shameful to some. One of the facts that is relevant here is that shaming people stimulates violence. Another is that providing people with the personal, cultural, and economic resources that strengthen their capacity to tolerate experiences of being shamed without resorting to violence is one way to prevent violence. While I have emphasized so far the pathogenic, maladaptive effects that exposure to feelings of shame can have, it is important to notice that shame can also serve an adaptive function, as an emotion that motivates us to overcome our areas of inferiority, correct our mistakes, and mature, develop, learn, acquire skills and accomplish things in which we can take pride and which can elicit respect from others. That can only happen, of course, when people have access to non-violent means of undoing shame and attaining a positive sense of self-worth, such as education and constructive, meaningful work. But when those conditions are in place, one measure of mental health can be defined as the ability to tolerate feelings of shame until one can replace them with feelings of pride by putting them to work in the service of stimulating growth, maturation, and constructive achievements, as opposed to the destructiveness of violence. When people do not have access to education and work, they may feel that the only means left to them by which to undo whatever feelings of shame they experience is violence.

We cannot grow and develop unless we can change, and we cannot change unless we can recognize that our old ways of thinking, feeling, and behaving have been limited, inadequate, or mistaken – inferior, if you will – and that we need to replace them with new ones that can do more to increase both our own ability to live fully and successfully, and that of our fellow human beings – on whom we depend, and who depend on us. One prerequisite for doing that is to develop the capacity to tolerate feelings of shame without resorting to violence as the means of diminishing them, so that we can benefit from the adaptive uses to which shame can be put, such as stimulating ambition, achievement and the acquisition of knowledge and skills.

One of the mistakes that leads to violence, I believe, is the tendency to divide individuals and groups into those that are all-good or all-bad. But my interest is in violence, and there, whether we like it or not, a clear and absolute binary does exist: namely, the difference between life and death. As a physician, I have devoted my life to attempting to save lives by identifying both the causes of death – the risk factors – and the protective factors, and attempting to remove or neutralize the pathogens and maximize the sources of healing. In looking at homicide and suicide rates, I did not expect to find myself engaged in a political and socio-economic analysis. I could explain individual cases of homicide or suicide from my clinical work with homicidal and suicidal individuals, focusing on the factors in their individual lives that predisposed them to kill others or themselves. It was the epidemics of violence that could not be explained simply by differences between individuals, since these changes from non-epidemic to epidemic rates and back again occurred within short periods of time within the same population.

Prisons as sub-cultures of shame and violence

For the past 40 years, I have been able to use prisons and jails as my social-psychological laboratory, so to speak, in which to learn about the causes and prevention of violence wherever it occurs and on whatever scale, in somewhat the same way that microbiology laboratories can enable us to learn about the causes of death as they operate in the community, outside the laboratory. Doctors in the nineteenth century discovered that the only way to end epidemics of infectious diseases was to change the environmental sources of pathogens to which everyone in the community was exposed, by, for example, cleaning up the water supply and the sewer system (and they only knew why that worked because of what they had learned in their laboratories). In my work in the prisons, I discovered that the only way to end the epidemic levels of suicide and homicide that were going on in these confined spaces was to change the culture in which every individual in the prison community was living and to which everyone was exposed.

What my colleagues and I did, first in the prisons of Massachusetts and then in the jails of San Francisco, was to search for ways to change an authoritarian shame culture into an egalitarian culture. This is not the place to take the space to describe the means by which we pursued that goal[18] except to say that the underlying principle was to treat everyone in the environment with respect and expect them to do the same, one means of doing which was to pay close attention to everyone and listen to their story with undivided attention, and to provide everyone with some non-violent means of gaining some greater degree of self-respect, such as education and meaningful work.

I began my violence-prevention work first in the prisons of Massachusetts, and then was able to develop and

---

[18] For a more detailed explanation of this experiment, see James Gilligan and Bandy Lee, "The Resolve to Stop the Violence Project: Reducing Violence in the Community through a Jail-Based Initiative," *Journal of Public Health*, 27(2): 143–8, June 2005; Bandy Lee and James Gilligan, "The Resolve to Stop the Violence Project: Transforming an In-House Culture of Violence through a Jail-Based Programme," *Journal of Public Health*, 27(2):149–55, June 2005; James Gilligan and Bandy Lee, "Beyond the Prison Paradigm: From Provoking Violence to Preventing It by Creating 'Anti-Prisons' (Residential Colleges and Therapeutic Communities)," in John Devine, James Gilligan, Klaus A. Miczek, Rashid Shaikh, and Donald Pfaff, eds., *Youth Violence: Scientific Approaches to Prevention*, *Annals of the New York Academy of Sciences*, 1036: 300–24, 2004; Sunny Schwartz (with David Boodell), *Dreams from the Monster Factory: A Tale of Prison, Redemption and One Woman's Fight to Restore Justice to All* (with an Introduction by James Gilligan), New York: Scribner, 2009.

refine it further in the jails of San Francisco. Throughout the 1970s, there had been a homicide a month and a suicide every six weeks in one 600–man Massachusetts prison alone, and riots, hostage-taking, and murders of staff, inmates, and visitors were occurring in the other prisons as well. Yet we were able, by the mid-1980s, to go for a year at a time with no lethal violence through-out the entire 12,000-man prison system.

I was then able to apply and test what we had learned from that experience in a more systematic way when the sheriff of the City and County of San Francisco, a lawyer named Michael Hennessey, wanted to replace retributive justice (which I would call a fancy term for revenge) with restorative justice (by giving violent criminals an incentive and a method of becoming agents of violence prevention, and thus giving back to the community something of what they had taken from it). Sunny Schwartz, Sheriff Hennessey's program director and also a lawyer, assembled a team of creative and innovative people, and my research partner, Dr. Bandy Lee, and I worked with them on the design, imple-mentation, and evaluation of an intensive, controlled violence-prevention experiment, which continued from 1997 to 2007.

One of the members of Sunny's team, Hamish Sinclair, had already developed a systematic method of decon-structing and reconstructing what he called the "male role belief system," meaning the whole set of assump-tions and values that almost all men in our society are taught in one form or another: namely, that the world is divided into two groups, the superior and the inferior; that in that dichotomy men are superior to women and real men are superior to other men; and that unless they enforce their superiority, if necessary by means of violence, they are by definition inferior and not even masculine. All those assumptions, which made up a type of shame ethic, are of course recipes for violence, which, as I said, was rampant in the prison culture until we worked intensively with the entire population of one dormitory (rather than cell-block) unit at a time to help them deconstruct and reconstruct the moral value system that serves as the ethos of a shame culture, i.e., what some criminologists have called a "sub-culture of violence."[19]

We found that the level of violence within the San Francisco jail, among those who were exposed to this experimental program, dropped to zero for an entire 12 months (whereas violence continued unchanged in a "control group" of prisoners in an ordinary jail, 60 percent of whom in any given year committed assaults that could have been prosecuted as felonies outside the jail); and that, upon release back into the community, the rate of violent recidivism, or reoffending with a new violent crime, during the first year, was 83 percent lower than in a matched control group that had been in an ordinary jail – after no more than 4 months of participation in this program.

From all these experiences, and my work as a consultant on prison violence around the world, I have concluded that it is possible to stop epidemics of violence, but that one can do so only by changing the culture in

[19] Marvin E. Wolfgang and Franco Ferracuti, *The Sub-Culture of Violence*, Beverly Hills, CA: Sage Publications, 1982.

which the population is living. Of course, we worked as intensively as we could with as many individuals as we could, and did so at least briefly with everyone, in our effort to enable us and them to understand and end their violence. But the key to ending the epidemic of violence was to change the social system – the cultural ocean, so to speak, in which all the fish swam.

My work in Massachusetts and San Francisco can hardly be said to have constituted more than a couple of isolated "pilot projects" in the prisons of one state and the jails of one city. But the purpose of pilot projects is to learn lessons that can then be applied on a larger scale outside the walls inside which they took place (and we have been replicating these projects in jails and prisons around the world, from New Zealand and Singapore to Poland and New York). I regard my work in these two quite different correctional settings, in Massachusetts and San Francisco, as experimental confirmations of the hypothesis that the value system that I have called here a shame ethic, and the socio-cultural system that I have called a shame culture (both of which valorize and maximize inequality, social status hierarchies, domination, and authoritarianism), stimulate violence of all types; and that dismantling those beliefs and practices and replacing them with an egalitarian, democratic set of social relationships, in which everyone treats everyone with equal respect regardless of their role in the group, is an effective means of preventing violence.

This experiment provided at least provisional confirmation of my hypothesis that when you challenge inequality (the division of a population into those who are superior to others and those who are inferior), you are striking at the violence-provoking heart of a shame culture, its capacity to induce the feelings and fears of inferiority to others that provoke violence (especially when people are deprived of non-violent means by which to attain feelings of pride, self-respect, and self-worth, such as education and work). We saw in the prisons what happened when a population consisting of the most violent men our society produces were given the opportunity to acquire a college education; and we see both in the prisons and in society as a whole what happens when people are deprived of the opportunity to engage in meaningful, remunerative work.

My intention in this book, then, is to extend and apply what we learned from this experiment in those microcosms of murder (and suicide) called prisons and jails to the macrocosm of our society as a whole. The fact that American society is plagued by recurrent epidemics of violence, and that even in its non-epidemic periods it has a level of violence far higher than those of the other developed nations of the world, underscores the urgency of this experiment. The fact that rates of suicide as well as of homicide are affected by the political, economic, and cultural forces I have described makes the results of this experiment more generally applicable.

It is important to stress that neither shame nor guilt is necessarily pathogenic, nor is the behavior they motivate always maladaptive. The challenge we face is to make available to everyone, inside and outside the prisons, the tools and resources they need in order to reduce their feelings of shame and augment their feelings of pride and self-worth by constructive and creative means, such as education and meaningful work, not destructive ones such as violence.

Conclusion: The Mystery Solved: What Is To Be Done?

I began with a mystery: a correlation that seemed to defy explanation. How could the political party of the president be among the causes of murder, whether of oneself or others? In the chapters of this book, I have laid out a causal chain that is capable of explaining the correlation and thus solving the mystery.

It took many years to establish the link between cigarette smoking and lung cancer. There was clearly an association but causation remained in dispute, in part because the cigarette companies invested huge amounts of money in their effort to cast doubt on the research findings.[1] Nevertheless, the International Agency for Research on Cancer has come up with seven criteria that they conclude can establish beyond reasonable doubt whether a given agent (e.g. cigarettes) could be regarded as causing a given outcome (e.g. lung cancer). I will

[1] David Michaels, *Doubt Is Their Product: How Industry's Assault on Science Threatens Your Health*, Oxford and New York: Oxford University Press, 2008.

use their seven criteria here to test whether the political party of the president, itself a proxy for a host of different social and economic policies, can similarly be regarded as causing increases or decreases in the level of lethal violence. To use public health terms, I am asking whether Republican administrations are a risk factor and whether Democratic administrations are a protective factor with respect to homicide and suicide.

In adopting the seven criteria laid out for cancer researchers, I follow them verbatim except that where they say cancer I say lethal violence, and where they speak of biological factors I speak of psychological and social factors.

1. The link or association between the exposure and lethal violence is strong. The association between exposure to political parties and violent death rates (suicide and homicide) is strong, consistent, and statistically significant. It is only when Republicans are in the White House that the rates of suicide and homicide increase to epidemic levels, and only when Democrats are in the White House that they decrease below these levels. This association occurs repeatedly and without any significant long-term exceptions over a wide variety of different time frames of differing lengths and social circumstances. Even more to the point, the net cumulative totals of suicide and homicide deaths from 1900 through 2007 show large and statistically significant increases during the years of Republican presidencies, and almost identical decreases during the Democratic administrations.

2. The risk of lethal violence increases with more expo-

sure to the agent. *The greater the number of years* of Republican administrations, the higher *the net cumulative increase* in rates of suicide and homicide. Conversely, *the greater the number of years* of Democratic administrations, the higher *the net cumulative decrease* in rates of suicide and homicide. That is, the higher the dose, the greater the response.

3. Multiple studies by different investigators with different groups of people come to the same finding. Although several of the sub-findings have been reported by other investigators, the main thesis of this book has not been proposed before. It is an original observation and one that I hope and trust others will seek to replicate. For the moment, suffice it to say that investigators in Australia and the United Kingdom have, independently of each other and of me, found that suicide rates increased significantly throughout the twentieth century in both countries when conservative political parties were in power, and decreased under liberal governments; and that the unemployment rate correlated both with the political parties and with the suicide rate.[2]

4. The exposure to the agent came before the violence. The net increases in suicide and homicide to epidemic levels occur only after Republicans are elected

---

[2] A. Page, S. Morrell, and R. Taylor, "Suicide and Political Regime in New South Wales and Australia during the 20th Century," *Journal of Epidemiological Community Health*, 56: 766–72, 2002; M. Shaw, D. Dorling, and G. Davey Smith, "Mortality and Political Climate: How Suicide Rates Have Risen during Periods of Conservative Government, 1901–2000," *Journal of Epidemiological Community Health*, 56: 723–5, 2002.

to the White House, and the net decreases below epidemic levels occur after Democrats are. While this does not prove the hypothesis ("after this" does not entail "because of this"), it is important to remember that the hypothesis could and would have been disconfirmed if the data had shown that the epidemics of violence occurred *before* Republicans came to power, and the resolution of the epidemics *before* the Democrats did. While events that occur *after* some other event are not necessarily caused by it, events that occur *before* some other event cannot be caused by it. Thus, we can say that this analysis represents an attempt to *disconfirm* the hypothesis, as recommended by Karl Popper,[3] and that it failed to do so. Or, to put it another way, the hypothesis as it stands is consistent with the observed chronological relationships between the hypothesized cause and the hypothesized effect.

5. There is a plausible psychological and social explanation for how the agent would cause the violence. Plausible social and psychological explanations for how Republican and Democratic presidencies act as "risk" and "protective" factors, respectively, in the multi-determined etiology of violent behavior have been discussed in previous chapters. To recapitulate, the immediate psychological motive, or cause, of violent behavior in individuals is exposure to overwhelming intensities of shame and humiliation (feelings of failure and inferiority, of being disrespected, rejected, held in contempt, and regarded as

---

[3] *The Logic of Scientific Discovery*, London: Hutchinson, 1959.

worthless, of no value to others, "redundant," etc.); these feelings can be stimulated and exacerbated by many stressors in the social environment, one of the most powerful and common of which is the experience of being fired from one's job, or for any other reason suffering a severe loss of socio-economic status; this experience has been more frequent and prolonged under Republican than under Democratic administrations throughout the twentieth century, and compensatory measures to reduce the intensity of the humiliation (e.g. the WPA under Roosevelt) have been more extensive and effective under Democratic than under Republican presidents.

6. The link is specific and the agent causes a specific type of lethal injury, namely intentional injury. What I am proposing in this book is that the two political parties have diametrically opposite effects on the causation or prevention of specific types of life-threatening or death-inducing pathology, namely, intentional lethal violence, i.e., homicide and suicide. There does not seem to be a similar correlation between the political parties and overall death rates in America from all causes, nor with the parties and the rates of accidental death. Overall death rates tend to fall every year as medicine advances, and since medical knowledge, once acquired, is, in principle, never lost but only accumulates and grows, it does not fluctuate around a mean from year to year as intentional violence does: it almost always moves only in one direction, toward ever-increasing life expectancies. Presidential elections are therefore likely to have only the most remote connection, if any, to the everyday practice

of medicine and medical knowledge. Also, any given research project of the type that is responsible for the growth of medical knowledge often takes years to complete and can easily overlap with more than one president without being affected by which party they belong to. Similarly, the yearly incidence of lethal unintentional injuries – the so-called "accidental" deaths – has tended to fall in almost all years since those rates began being measured in 1900. What this demonstrates is that, if there is one thing that is not accidental, it is so-called "accidents," most of which are preventable – so they in fact have been prevented progressively more effectively, and the preventive techniques, such as automobile seat belts, motorcycle helmets, and so on, once adopted, tend not to be abandoned. Rather, they continue to be preserved and make a permanent contribution to safety, so that, as with medicine, there tends to be cumulative progress in preventing "accidental" deaths, rather than the wide fluctuations in death rates that one sees with intentional injuries.

7. The link fits together with what we know from other studies. Every link in the causal chain presented here fits together with findings from other research studies. Both the correlation between political parties and violent death rates, and the interlocking chain of causal mechanisms that explain that correlation, fit together with what we know from other studies of: (a) the association between political parties and numerous forms of *socio-economic stress, distress, and inequality* – including rates and duration of unemployment; depth, duration, and frequency of

economic contractions, recessions, and depression; inequalities of wealth and income, i.e., relative poverty and deprivation – all of which have been shown in social-scientific studies to increase statistically under Republicans and decrease under Democrats; (b) the association between *relative economic stress*, deprivation or inferiority, including economic inequality, unemployment, economic growth, and *lethal violence*, which has been confirmed and reconfirmed in multiple published studies, and is indeed one of the most robust findings in the social-scientific literature; (c) the fact that the experience of becoming *unemployed* or suffering any other major sudden loss of socio-economic status (e.g. being rejected, and defined as worthless and valueless by one's employer) and thereby subjected to a lowering of one's socio-economic status, leads to increased intensities of *shame and humiliation*; (d) the causal association between feelings of overwhelming *shame and humiliation* and *violent behavior* – suicide and homicide – has been reported and replicated in every branch of the behavioral sciences, and has indeed, for centuries and millennia, been one of the most ancient and widely repeated observations about human behavior.

As cigarette smoking has been shown to increase the rates of lung cancer, so the presence of a Republican in the White House increases the rates of suicide and homicide. And as regular exercise and drinking red wine in moderation have been shown to increase longevity, so the presence of a Democrat in the White House decreases the incidence of lethal violence. Not everyone who smokes gets lung cancer; not every Republican president presides over an epidemic of lethal violence. Not everyone who exercises lives a long and healthy life; not every Democratic president presides over a decrease in violence. What I have demonstrated here is a highly significant link between the party affiliation of the president and the rate of lethal violence in the society, and I have solved the mystery posed by this correlation by identifying a chain of evidence that can explain what is otherwise an inexplicable association.

I want to discuss the larger implications of these findings both for American politics and for the understanding of violence, but, first, I can sum them up with two syllogisms, the premises of which are based on empirical evidence.

The first syllogism is the psychological syllogism:

Major premise: Feelings of shame and humiliation motivate, and hence increase the rates of, both suicide and homicide.

Minor premise: Socio-economic distress and suffering in the form of unemployment, relative poverty and the sudden loss of social and economic status stimulate feelings of shame and humiliation.

Conclusion: Therefore, socio-economic distress and suffering, in the forms just mentioned, increase the rates of suicide and homicide.

(Empirical evidence in support of the major and minor premises and the conclusion are summarized in chapters 4, 5, and 2, respectively.)

The second syllogism is the political syllogism:

Major premise: Republican administrations increase the level of socio-economic distress and Democratic administrations reduce them.

Minor premise: Economic and social distress increase rates of homicide and suicide.

Conclusion: Therefore, suicide and homicide rates can be expected to increase during Republican administrations and decrease under Democratic ones.

(Empirical evidence in support of the major and minor premises and the conclusion are summarized in chapters 3, 2 and 1, respectively.)

Implications for the future of American politics

By now, it should be obvious that it is not the party label as such that causes changes in the rates of lethal violence. Instead, the party label is merely a proxy for thousands of policies and practices carried out by thousands of people who come to power in any given administration. But, beneath all the variability from one president and one party to another, it turns out that there is enough continuity and consistency associated with each party label for certain statistical regularities to emerge. Or, to vary the metaphor, each party and each administration can be seen as a package containing many different ingredients, some toxic and some salubrious for public health, social and mental (as measured by rates of suicide and homicide), just as cigarettes are a package containing a variety of ingredients that add to

163

their lethality, and regular exercise is a package containing a variety of ingredients that prolong life.

The implication of the research reported here for American politics is rather stark: the Republican party functions as a risk factor for lethal violence and the Democratic party functions as a protective factor.

Having said this, I want now to broaden the lens and make a distinction between political democracy and social democracy. Political democracy, which is common to the United States and all other developed countries, has been shown in many studies to prevent international violence between democracies. However, social democracies, which exist in every developed country except the United States, have been shown in virtually all studies of this subject to decrease the form of intranational violence called homicide. The United States stands alone in maintaining a rate of murder that would be considered, even at its lowest levels, an epidemic in every one of the other developed countries. The way I understand this is in terms of the continuing prevalence and political influence of a shame ethic and shame cultures within the United States, which determine political and economic values and assumptions.

Looking at the current state of American politics, the antagonism between Republicans and Democrats and the divisions between Red and Blue States, we can see a polarization that has never been higher. To those who say, as Ralph Nader did from the left and as George Wallace did from the right, that there is no difference between Republicans and Democrats, I would respond that the data presented in this book show that things are not quite that simple. In this book I am concentrating almost exclusively on domestic policy because I am attempting to understand a domestic outcome – intra-national violence, not international. So I will not even comment here on comparisons between the Democrats' and the Republicans' foreign or military policies. But even when looking only at domestic actions, I have to admit that, yes, it is true that Democrats often do the will of their corporate masters – how else could they persuade them to donate the campaign funds without which they could not win any elections? For example, under Clinton, economic inequality continued to increase, which it had been doing since – and only since – the Republicans ended the 37-year period of Democratic hegemony that had lasted from 1933 until Nixon took office in 1969. But this inequality was increasing only about a third as fast under Clinton as it had been under Reagan and Bush Sr.[4] And there were many other indices of economic equality, which I have mentioned before, that did improve during Clinton's terms in office. But most importantly, for the purposes of this book, lethal violence rates during Democratic administrations going back to the beginning of the twentieth century had fallen, not risen (as they had done under the Republicans). In that respect, the two parties were not merely *different*, they were *opposite* to each other! The same applies to the rates and duration of unemployment, both of which have, like the rates of suicide and homicide, also increased during Republican

---

[4] Jared Bernstein, Lawrence Mishel, and Chauna Brocht, "Any Way You Cut It: Income Inequality on the Rise Regardless of How It's Measured," Briefing Paper, Economic Policy Institute, n.d. Downloaded from http://epinet.org.

administrations and decreased under Democratic ones. Again, not merely different – opposite.

And since the two parties have diametrically opposite effects on the rates of lethal violence, the choice between electing Republicans and Democrats to the White House is a choice between life and death, and not just one death but thousands of them, year after year.

The fact that lethal violence is the bell-wether directs our attention to the role of shame. Although it is not usually cast in these terms, the polarization rending US politics reflects a clash between an authoritarian shame ethic and a more egalitarian ethic that, at its highest stage of development, may have more to do with love, equal respect for self and others, and what Albert Schweitzer called "reverence for life," than with either shame or guilt.

And now I would like to turn to considering the implications the data presented in this book might have for the way we think about politics.

How to think about politics

The US Declaration of Independence states in its famous preamble that "All men are created equal," that "Governments are instituted among Men" in order to secure their "unalienable Rights" to "Life, Liberty and the pursuit of Happiness," and that "whenever any Form of Government" (or, by implication, any political party) "becomes destructive of these ends, it is the Right of the People to alter or to abolish it, and to institute new Government such . . . as to them shall seem most likely to effect their Safety and Happiness." The Constitution of the United States stated its purpose (and, by implication, the purpose of forming this new nation) was to "insure domestic tranquility . . . promote the general welfare, and secure the blessings of liberty to ourselves and our posterity."

If the data presented in this book are correct, it would seem difficult to avoid the conclusion that they constitute empirical evidence that, from 1900 through 2007, the Republican party has impeded and the Democratic party has facilitated our ability to achieve every single one of those goals for whose attainment the American government was created. For the effect of the Republican party has been to reduce, not maximize, the amount of equality, life, liberty, happiness, safety, domestic tranquility, and general welfare enjoyed by the American people. The Democratic party, through its leadership and policies, has had the opposite effect.

Jefferson issued a litany of charges against George III and the British government he headed. Following Jefferson's example, I will describe the Republican party in terms not dissimilar from those he used to characterize the British king.

1) *Equality*. They have increased – whereas the Democratic party has decreased – the degree of economic inequality among the American people. They have also increased, not decreased, racial inequality through a "Southern strategy" that resulted in their finally returning to power in 1969 by winning votes through appealing to the racial prejudices that are still widespread in the former slave states, and among

many whites in the rest of the country as well; by supporting discriminatory drug laws, law enforcement practices, and prison sentencing policies that have resulted in the disproportionate imprisonment of African-Americans; and by depriving millions of African-Americans, for the rest of their lives, of the right to vote, once they were convicted of any felony (for example, one violation of the drug laws, for which they are prosecuted far more often than whites, even though the rate at which those laws are broken by members of the two races is essentially the same). I cannot see how this pattern of interrelated policies can be understood except as the re-imposition of white supremacy by the Republican party, whether that was its conscious intention or not, after slavery, lynching, disenfranchisement by means of poll taxes and "literacy tests," and racial segregation had all been legally abolished at various different times over the past century and a half, and after the civil rights movement, Supreme Court decisions, and Kennedy's and Johnson's civil rights legislation threatened to undo the old patterns of racial inequality, once and for all.

2) *Life*. The Republican party has been a force destructive to life, to the extent that the effect of its governance has been to increase the rates of suicide and homicide, including capital punishment, not to decrease them as the Democrats and the Democratic majority Blue States have done.

3) *Liberty*. The ultimate deprivation of liberty is, of course, death, including by means of the death penalty, as well as murder and suicide; the second

greatest, imprisonment; the third greatest, the inability to travel where you want and do what you want without the fear of being assaulted or even killed. Republicans have reduced liberty to the extent that the "war on crime" initiated by President Nixon in 1968 led not only to the greatest increase in violent crime since the last previous period of Republican hegemony that culminated in the Great Depression, but also, and on a scale far greater than the increase in rates of crimes and violence, to a historically unprecedented explosion in the rate of incarceration, beginning in the mid-1970s. As a result of this, the US imprisonment rate is now higher than that of any other nation on earth, including such police states as China and Iran, and six to seven times higher than it was in the US at any time before the Republicans returned to power in 1969.

4) *The pursuit of happiness.* On the principle that actions speak louder than words, one of the most accurate measures of the degree of happiness in a society is its suicide and homicide rates. They are the tips of the icebergs of two types of unhappiness – with oneself and one's own life, as in suicide, and with other people and their lives, as in homicide. Thus, the Republican party's effectiveness in increasing the rates of both of these forms of lethal violence can be seen as empirical evidence of the degree to which they defeat rather than advance the pursuit of happiness (in contrast to the Democratic party's record in this regard).

5) *Safety and domestic tranquility.* If the degree of safety and domestic tranquility in a society can be

measured by the degree to which its citizens are free from the threat and reality of lethal violence, then it would be difficult to avoid the conclusion that the Republican party moves the US further from that goal also, in contrast to the Democratic party's record in that regard.

6) *The general welfare.* If the general welfare can be gauged in part by the degree to which people are economically secure (employed, with access to good education, housing, and health care, with incomes and wealth sufficient to shield them from both absolute and relative poverty and deprivation "from cradle to grave," and with the opportunity to live in a society with a flourishing economy), then the data presented in this book would seem to offer empirical evidence that it is the Democratic party that improves the chances of achieving every one of those goals, whereas the Republican party diminishes them. But perhaps the greatest irony is that the political rhetoric common to Republican politicians serves to distract people from awareness of those facts by accusing the Democrats of aiming at a European-style social democracy or "welfare state," and then claiming that that in turn would lead to Soviet-style communism, poverty, and tyranny. This argument represents an egregious distortion of reality, in that all the nations of Western Europe, without exception, since shortly after the Second World War, have formed themselves into remarkably non-violent, peaceful, prosperous welfare states with the same degree of political democracy and civil liberties as in the US but with much less poverty, homelessness, murder,

and imprisonment, no capital punishment, longer life spans, greater leisure, less infant and maternal mortality and morbidity, greater access to free, high-quality child care, health care, and higher education, and greater economic security than the people of the United States are able to enjoy.

In conclusion, I want to take up three questions: first, are there any other social, political, or economic variables that could explain away the data reported in this book? That is, could there be other causes of the changes documented here that would show that the correlations between the two political parties and the two violent death rates are spurious? Have we exhausted all possible attempts to disconfirm the hypothesis that there is a causal relationship between the nature of the two political parties and the violent death rates observed under each?

Did prisons bring down our lethal violence rates?

For example, was it the social engineering experiment called mass incarceration that actually brought down the rates of lethal violence under Clinton during the 1990s? If so, the Republicans should be given credit, since the policy of mass imprisonment occurred in response to Nixon's call in 1968 for a "war on crime" and a "war on drugs." And was it the "zero tolerance" and "broken windows" policing policies pursued by New York's Republican mayor Giuliani (during the years Clinton was president) that brought down the rates of suicide and homicide in New York City during that time? Was

New York unique among the major cities of that time, and a demonstration that only Republican political leaders know how to prevent violence and that they do it better than their Democratic rivals?

We can easily show that mass incarceration is not the explanation for the dramatic decrease in lethal violence that occurred only after Clinton was elected. The US suffered an epidemic of suicide and homicide that began in Nixon's second year in office (1970) and lasted without interruption throughout four Republican administrations and one Democratic one (Carter's). When Clinton took office in 1993, he inherited from his Republican predecessor, Bush Sr., a suicide rate of 11.3 and a homicide rate of 10.4 per 100,000 per year. By 1997, both of those rates had dropped below their epidemic "floors" (which, as I mentioned above, could be considered as 11 for suicide, 8 for homicide), thus bringing an end to the epidemic levels of violence that had been going on for the previous 27 years. By Clinton's last year in office, 2000, the homicide rate had declined from 10.4 to 6.4, the lowest level since 1966; and the suicide rate had dropped from 11.3 to 9.6, the lowest level since 1902.

Could that dramatic decrease in lethal violence have been caused by the equally dramatic increase in our imprisonment rate? If the increase in our prison population, beginning in the mid-1970s during Nixon's second term in office, were responsible for the ending of our epidemic of violence, why did it take until 1997 to bring the epidemic to an end?

Our national imprisonment rate had been essentially constant throughout the first three-quarters of the twentieth century at roughly 100 (plus or minus 20) per 100,000 population. It was only in the mid-1970s that it began increasing steadily and rapidly year after year so that today it is over 700 per 100,000. Is there any evidence that this prison-building and prison-stuffing binge was even indirectly responsible for ending the epidemic of violence? Here is some relevant evidence that it was not:

1) Since our epidemic of violence involves suicide as well as homicide, it is worth noticing that not even the most avid supporters of mass imprisonment claim that there is any reason to believe that increasing our incarceration rate would have in any way contributed to the decline in the suicide rate that occurred following Clinton's election. In fact, imprisonment is well known as a major precipitant of suicide, not as a preventer of it.

2) Two Democratic presidents, Woodrow Wilson and Franklin Roosevelt, both inherited epidemics of lethal violence from their Republican predecessors (in 1913 and 1933, respectively), and succeeded in ending those epidemics without making any major increases in the incarceration rate. That is consistent with the conclusion that increasing the imprisonment rate is not a *necessary* prerequisite for ending an epidemic of violence.

3) The series of Republican presidents from Nixon to Bush Sr. (1969–92) began by inheriting a non-epidemic rate of lethal violence from their Democratic predecessors, Kennedy and Johnson, and turned it, from 1970 on, into the longest uninterrupted epidemic of lethal violence in the twentieth century, despite increasing the imprisonment rate from

roughly 100 to 700 per 100,000, for the first and only time in the twentieth century. That increase did not have the slightest effect on the homicide rate, which remained continuously at epidemic levels. That is consistent with the conclusion that increases in the imprisonment rate are not *sufficient* for ending an epidemic of violence.

4) A Democratic president, Bill Clinton, inherited the epidemic of lethal violence left him by his Republican predecessors in 1993, and ended the epidemic without ending the ongoing yearly increase in imprisonment rates.

5) Wilson, Roosevelt, and Clinton all inherited epidemics not only of violence but also of unemployment (and other indices of socio-economic inequality, stress, and deprivation) from their Republican predecessors, and ended those epidemics as well.

6) The net implication of all the empirical evidence cited in the above five paragraphs would seem to be that increasing the imprisonment rate (as the Republicans did) is neither necessary nor sufficient for either preventing or ending epidemics of lethal violence; but that ending epidemics of unemployment and relative deprivation (as the Democrats did) is both necessary and sufficient for preventing and ending epidemics of lethal violence.

As the National Academy of Sciences' review of this question concluded in 1993:

What effect has increasing the prison population had on levels of violent crime? Apparently, very little. . . .

If tripling the average length of incarceration per crime had a strong preventive effect, then violent crime rates should have declined. . . . Analyses suggest that a further increase in the average time served per violent crime would have an even smaller proportional incapacitation effect than the increase [in time served] that occurred between 1975 and 1989. . . . This analysis suggests that *preventive* strategies may be as important as criminal justice *responses* to violence.[5]

In fact, I must turn the question around and ask whether our policy of mass incarceration might have had exactly the reverse effect. After all, prisons have been known throughout the centuries as "schools for crime" – in fact, graduate schools in crime and violence, or, as my colleague Sunny Schwartz[6] has called them, "monster factories." We have only been able to fill all the prisons we have built, to the point of severely over-crowding them, by sentencing an ever larger number of people to them for non-violent crimes. And, as I have repeatedly observed over the past 40 years and as all recidivism statistics demonstrate, the most effective way to turn a non-violent person into a violent one is to send him to prison. So we have to ask whether putting more and more non-violent people into prisons for longer and longer times might actually have had the effect of prolonging and exacerbating our epidemic of violence, rather than of mitigating or ending it; and whether

---

[5] Albert J. Reiss Jr. and Jeffrey A. Roth, eds. (Panel on the Understanding and Control of Violent Behavior, National Research Council, National Academy of Sciences), *Understanding and Preventing Violence*, Vol. I, Washington, DC: National Academy Press, 1993.

[6] Schwartz, *Dreams from the Monster Factory*.

the dramatic and rapid reduction in lethal violence rates that occurred during the Clinton administration (1993–2000) occurred *despite* the continuing orgy of mass incarceration, rather than because of it.

One last piece of evidence that the policy of mass incarceration had no demonstrable effect on the murder rate is the fact that, in 1970, when our national incarceration rate was about where it had been for the first three-quarters of the twentieth century – 100 per 100,000 population – the murder rate was 8.3 per 100,000. By 15 years later, in 1985, the incarceration rate had doubled to about 200 per 100,000. What was the murder rate? Still 8.3. By another 11 years after that, in 1996, the imprisonment rate had doubled again to more than 400 per 100,000. What was the murder rate that year? Still 8.3. It does not appear that the doubling or even quadrupling of the imprisonment rate over a 27–year period made even the slightest dent in the murder rate, which came down below the epidemic "floor" of 8 (in fact, reaching a low of 6.4 by 2000) only after President Clinton had instituted the economic reforms described in this book; following which, with the election of another Republican president, Bush Jr., the murder rate immediately stopped declining and reversed itself, drifting upward even though (or perhaps because) the imprisonment rate also continued to climb upward.

Is Giuliani the one?

But what about New York's Mayor Giuliani? Didn't he bring New York's epidemic of violent crime under control by getting "tough on crime" with his no-nonsense, "zero tolerance" policy for any violations of the law, even ones as trivial as failing to pay a subway fare? Let me begin by referring to what I said above: not even Giuliani's most avid supporters would claim that "getting tough on crime" could have had any noticeable effect on the suicide rate, which also declined, not just in New York but also throughout the nation, during Giuliani's years in office. Clearly, something more was going on in every major city in the country than just Giuliani's policy of a more inflexible punitiveness toward the most trivial of crimes – and in many cases what was going on was the opposite of Giuliani's policies, which was nevertheless followed by comparable reductions in both homicide and suicide.

Giuliani was the mayor of New York during 1994–2001, almost exactly the same years during which Clinton was president of the United States (1993–2000), and, as I have said, the murder rate throughout the country began declining dramatically year by year, from 10.5 during Clinton's first year in office, to 6.4 by his last. During those years, the murder rate declined equally dramatically in every one of the 25 largest cities in the United States – not just New York, but every one. And they did this while pursuing policies that were in some cases the opposite of New York's. San Diego, California, for example, the fifth-largest city in the country, had a decline in its homicide rate that was not significantly different from New York's, but their police, rather than getting "tougher" on their citizens, enlisted them as allies by forming a cooperative working relationship with neighborhood "crime watch" groups.

While New York's murder rate decline was the largest in percentage terms of the largest cities, the percentage increase in its murder rate during the previous 35 years had been among the highest. For example, between 1960 and 1990, the national homicide rate increased by 117 percent, whereas New York City's increased by 368 percent. New York's murder epidemic began and ended on approximately the same schedule as the nation's, with the non-epidemic period lasting until the late 1960s, epidemic levels from 1970 on, and a year-by-year decline back down to normal levels during the Clinton years of the 1990s. It both increased and decreased at faster rates than the nation's did, but it did so on essentially the same schedule, as did the murder rates in all of the largest cities. So, despite the enormous positive publicity Mayor Giuliani succeeded in gaining for himself, a review of the actual history of what happened leaves one reminded of the rooster who thought it was his crowing that made the sun rise. As the criminologist Andrew Karmen put it, "It appears that New York's [police] commissioners have pointed to forces beyond their control when the situation was deteriorating [i.e., when the homicide rate was skyrocketing, during the years of national Republican hegemony] and have accepted full responsibility when conditions were getting better." And the same appears to be true of the city's mayor.

To summarize, then, another reason for doubting that it was mass imprisonment rather than the election of a Democratic president that helped end our epidemic of lethal violence is the fact that all three epidemics of lethal violence in the twentieth century ended not with the introduction of mass imprisonment, but with the election of a Democratic president: Woodrow Wilson in 1912, Franklin Roosevelt in 1932, and Bill Clinton in 1992. All of those presidents inherited epidemics of lethal violence from their Republican predecessors, and all three epidemics ended without changes in the imprisonment rate (or, in Clinton's case, without changing the pattern of ongoing year-by-year increases in the imprisonment rate that had already been going on throughout the previous quarter of a century without any decline in rates of either homicide or suicide, and continued even after Clinton left office). All of those Democratic presidents did, however, undertake many policies that had the effect of reducing economic inequality, for example substantially increasing the progressivity of income and other taxes (e.g. increasing the highest marginal income tax rates), reducing the rate and duration of unemployment, increasing the social-welfare "safety net" for the poorest and most vulnerable members of the population, and increasing general prosperity and economic growth and expansion.

The resemblance between the Roosevelt and Clinton records with respect to lethal violence rates is especially close. Rates of both suicide and homicide began declining dramatically and steeply, year after year, beginning with the first year of their administrations for suicide and the second year for homicides, and both brought those rates below epidemic levels by the beginning of their second term in office, with the decreases continuing right up to their last year in office. It is well known how active Roosevelt was in sponsoring innumerable policies, laws, and agencies to undo the Great

Depression that began under the Republicans. One result was that the economy reversed from one of contraction to one of expansion, beginning in Roosevelt's first year in office (as the National Bureau of Economic Research has shown), so that, while it took World War II to bring a definitive end to the Depression, the fact is that Roosevelt began mitigating and undoing it right from the beginning. But, perhaps just as important with respect to matters like suicide and homicide, he also succeeded in enabling millions of people throughout the country who were in despair and felt abandoned by their government and the other institutions of their society to feel cared about and to become capable of a renewed sense of hope.

While all that is well known about Roosevelt, it is not as well known that the rates of suicide and homicide reached the lowest levels in 30 years by Clinton's fifth year in office (1997) only when the unemployment rate had also reached the lowest level in 30 years; both median and minimum wages had increased in real terms for the first time in 30 years (despite Republican Congressional leaders' opposition to the latter); the "negative income tax" (the Earned Income Tax Credit), which most economists believe is the most effective poverty-prevention tool in our economic arsenal, was given an unprecedented increase (thus undoing the Republican attempt to abolish it entirely); and the proportion of families in two of the demographic groups most vulnerable to homicidal violence – African-Americans and Latinos – whose incomes were below the poverty level declined to the lowest percentages since those indices first began being measured. Clinton has often been depicted by liberal Democrats as a "Republicrat" and has been accused of having compromised with the Republicans to the point where there was little difference left between the two parties (as when he agreed to "dismantle the welfare system as we know it" and to make work a precondition for some forms of welfare). But the US president whom he most resembles with respect to the matters that are the subject of this book is Roosevelt, the only other president who did as much as Clinton to undo both an epidemic of Republican-caused violence, and an economic structure of Republican-caused inequality and relative poverty.

Thus I find it difficult to conclude that the policy of mass incarceration that was initiated under a Republican president, Nixon, can plausibly be believed to have ended the epidemic of lethal violence that also began during his administration. By contrast, there are multiple reasons for believing that the very different policies pursued by a Democratic president were responsible for ending that epidemic, because there are multiple causal mechanisms, at the level of social and economic affairs and at the level of individual emotional and psychological health and welfare (the restoration of pride, hope, confidence, and the sense that one lives in a society that cares about one's welfare), that can plausibly be seen as mediating between the two variables whose correlation we are studying here – the rate of lethal violence, and the political party that is in power.

I have now presented you with my candidate for a solution to the murder mystery by uncovering the causal links connecting the political party of the occupant of the White House to the rates of lethal violence. But I have also discovered why it is a mystery, or rather needs to be a mystery: i.e., why these facts have been hiding in plain sight for the past century. It becomes clear now that the "divide and conquer" strategy extends to the division between homicide and suicide – because "they" commit homicide and "we," or at least the more unfortunate of us, commit suicide instead. We can now see why it seems so important not to see the violence in suicide, and thus to place killing oneself in the universe of mental illness and killing others in the universe of crime and violence. For this keeps us from making the connection between both forms of lethal violence and the political and economic system. In the end, it is no mystery why this murder mystery has been a mystery.

I began this journey by looking at data that were of interest to me as someone invested in uncovering the causes of violence. The data themselves are arcane – statistics compiled by the National Center for Health Statistics. The fact that suicide and homicide rates rise and fall together was of interest to me, as were the mountain peak and valley patterns of their distribution across the twentieth century – the fact that there were periods when these rates rose to epidemic levels and other times when they returned to what might be thought of as "normal." When I spotted on the correspondence between these peaks and valleys and the presidential election cycle, I literally could not believe my eyes.

And even now, some years since I first observed the association and found it to be a statistically significant correlation, I have a sense of crossing a boundary in moving from the consideration of violent deaths, whether self-inflicted or inflicted by others, to issues of political parties and social justice. And I wonder if others share this sense of transgression. Not only in seeing something that is not meant to be seen, but also of crossing categories.

It is painful enough to think about suicide or about murder when it occurs not on the movie screen but in somebody's life. The categories we have set up for thinking about these tragic events are those of mental illness and criminology, respectively. In this book, the murder and suicide rates became flags, like nautical markers showing a channel that led not into the heart of the despondent individual or murderer but into the White House and the economic policies that differentiate our two major political parties. Some politicians are more dangerous than others, not because they are bad people or because they never do good, but because the policies they pursue cause death.

Is it the president or the party?

One of the most important and perhaps most surprising implications of the data presented in this book is that the party of the president appears to be an even more powerful predictor and determinant of the rise and fall of lethal violence epidemics, and such closely associated economic phenomena as unemployment, inequality, and overall prosperity (the rate of economic growth), than the personality of the individual president himself. I emphasize that because most presidential election campaigns seem to me to be treated by the candidates, the mass media, and the general voting public as a kind of "beauty contest" or "horse race" between two individuals who just happen to be the candidates of one party or the other – as though it is the difference between the personalities or the biographies of the two individuals that is the most important basis for deciding whom to vote for. That may be especially true for those voters who regard themselves as "independents," rather than those who already have a firm partisan identity and always vote for "their" party's candidate. On the other hand, it is usually the independent swing voters, as well as those who switch their vote from the candidate of the party they usually support to that of the other party, who determine the outcome of many elections. Thus, I believe it is important to emphasize the fact that, despite the rather large differences in personality between the 12 Republican presidents and the 7 Democratic ones who served between 1900 and 2007, it was the party label that predicted their effect on lethal violence far more clearly than did any identifiable differences between the individuals. After all, who could be more different from each other than the flamboyant Teddy Roosevelt and the phlegmatic William Howard Taft, or the dour Richard Nixon and the sunny-dispositioned Ronald Reagan, or the patrician Franklin Roosevelt and that commonest of common men, Harry Truman? And yet the party affiliation clearly overrode each of those individual differences, and united the most disparate of personalities under the banner of a common party.

So it is important for voters to remember that when they vote for a presidential candidate, they are not voting for an individual nearly as much as they are voting for a political party, and for all the associated baggage, for good or for ill, that goes with that party. I realize that may sound like the father who thinks he is giving good advice when he advises his child that you don't marry an individual, you marry a family (advice that, in my experience, those who are in love with an individual do not want to hear, since they are in love with the individual, not his or her family). But whether or not that is good advice regarding marriage, I think that it is valuable for voters to remember, when deciding whom to vote for, that it is, with extremely rare exceptions (only Eisenhower, among the 12 Republican presidents from 1900 to 2007, and Carter, among the 7 Democrats, had records that were even slightly atypical for presidents from their party), more important to notice the difference between the parties of the candidates than the difference between the individual candidates themselves. Indeed, one purpose of framing an election campaign as a purely individual contest between the two candidates may be to distract the voting public from noticing what the actual policies of their parties are, so that the debate is over two individuals and whatever personal accomplishments or scandals they are associated with, rather than over the consequences of their parties' policies and political and economic records.

Another implication of the data presented here is that much – if not most – political rhetoric, both during an election campaign and during the actual governing and legislative process that follows the election, is so much hot air, since it consists of speculations, predictions, and unsupported opinions as to which party's policies are going to be more effective in increasing life, liberty, happiness, safety, domestic tranquility, prosperity, and welfare – in the future, after a particular bill is passed, or a particular individual elected. But what the data presented here show is that, with regard to most issues, we do not need to speculate about the future, for we already know what the past has shown us – namely, that it is Republican policies that have repeatedly, regularly, and with remarkable consistency brought us large increases in the rate and duration of unemployment, in the frequency, depth, and duration of recessions and depressions, in socio-economic inequalities in wealth and income, and in rates of suicide, homicide, and (since the mid-1970s) imprisonment and capital punishment; and it is Democratic policies that have brought us equally large decreases in all of those destructive phenomena (even in imprisonment and capital punishment, as the contrast between the Red and Blue States shows).

What surprised me most in writing this book was the discovery that the rates of lethal violence were like a string hanging out of a maze, and that, by following the string, I was led through a series of turns past the economic and social policies of Republican and Democratic administrations, the psychology of shame and guilt, the association of shame with unemployment (redundancy) and socio-economic inferiority, and the polarization of American politics into Red and Blue States.

I am a physician, not an economist or political scientist. My interest, training, and experience have focused on matters of life and death, not recessions and elections – and especially on the causes and prevention of violent death, which I have approached as problems in public health and preventive medicine, including preventive psychiatry. I was as surprised as anyone when my investigations of the causes and prevention of the deaths caused by violence led me, quite unexpectedly, to the discovery that certain political and economic phenomena could play an etiological role in the pathogenesis of life-threatening behavior, functioning as "risk factors"; and that certain others could play a preventive or even therapeutic role, as "protective factors."

In the end, I arrived at the realization that the association of rates of lethal violence with the party to which the occupant of the Oval Office belonged could be explained by the nesting of Republican and Democratic parties with social and economic policies that fostered or alleviated inequality, respectively, with the contrast between shame and guilt ethics, and the contrast between authoritarian (shame-driven) and egalitarian personalities and cultures.

In the end, then, I began to think that the maze itself tends to keep people from seeing this. However, by examining the rates of lethal violence we open a window into our political and economic system that makes it difficult for us not to see what we are doing. What I would ask you, my reader, is not to close this window too quickly, but rather to join me in thinking about two final questions.

What has made it so difficult or seemingly impossible for the Democrats to free themselves from Republican campaign rhetoric's reversal of the truth and take credit for their success in ending epidemics of lethal violence in this country for over a century? They, and they alone, have done this. Could this be the downside of being ruled by a guilt ethic and inhibiting their aggression so much that they, the Democrats, often fail to defend themselves strongly enough to undo both the misinformation and the damage caused by their Republican adversaries?

Second, following Thomas Jefferson's statement that it is "the Right of the People," whenever "any Form of Government becomes destructive" of the ends of life, liberty, and the pursuit of happiness, "to institute new Government such . . . as to them shall seem most likely to effect their Safety and Happiness," what actions might we now take with respect to our political parties in the service of this creative endeavor and in the interest of achieving "domestic tranquility" and advancing the "general welfare?" In the mid nineteenth century, the Republican party's predecessor, the Whig party, simply imploded and was replaced by a Republican party whose first and greatest president, Abraham Lincoln, achieved the most radically progressive, egalitarian and liberalizing reform in America's social and political history, the eradication of slavery. And the Republican party, after Lincoln's death, followed its great success in advancing democratic ideals by gradually reversing itself from being the party of progress and equality to being the party of reaction and inequality, from its egregious pandering to the "Robber Barons" which led to what Mark Twain called "the Gilded Age" at the end of the nineteenth century, to the "Southern strategy" through which the Republican party returned to power in 1969, at the cost of making itself the party of racial discrimination rather than racial equality.

The great question that confronts us now, I believe, is this: can we find non-violent means of replacing the

Republican party, which has become the main source of a degree of inequality and violence that the Democratic party has only partially reversed even when it was in power, with a party that could succeed in reducing inequality, relative poverty, and violence as much as has been done by the social-democratic parties of every other Western democracy? From Western Europe to Canada and Australasia, the rates of murder, imprisonment and relative poverty have been only 10–20 percent as high as in the US for most of the past 40 years. What would the United States look like if the Republican party went the way of its Whig predecessor and simply imploded, and the Democratic party's "loyal opposition" came from its left rather than from its right? Could the US finally become as humane and civilized as other Western democracies? To accomplish this would require confronting the shame ethic that renders social democracy a threat to those with a need for social stratification and hierarchy, and makes it shameful and politically risky for Democrats themselves to endorse more egalitarian social policies.

Another implication of the data summarized here is that, insofar as we are trying to prevent lethal violence, by reducing the rates of suicide and homicide on a nationwide scale, it is far more important to identify, also on a nationwide scale, the risk factors in our social, economic, and political environment that elevate, and the protective factors that reduce, the frequency with which individuals commit those actions, than it is to merely identify which specific individuals are at greater or lesser risk of doing so, and offer them therapy (or imprisonment) only after they have already become exposed to those risk factors, or attempted or committed violent acts. Clinical medicine focuses on getting doctors and hospitals and medicines to heal individual patients after they have become sick. And while we will always need that option, since even the best preventive medicine is almost never 100 percent successful, what we need to emphasize far more strongly is approaching our epidemics of lethal violence from the orientation of public health and preventive medicine. In the nineteenth century we discovered that cleaning up the water supply and the sewer system is far more effective in preventing deaths than all the doctors, medicines, and hospitals in the world. In the twentieth century we learned that it is both less expensive and more effective to assure that food is uncontaminated than it is to treat salmonella infections after they occur.

In the same spirit, what we need to learn in the twenty-first century is that cleaning up our political and economic system, by reducing the inequality, humiliation, and despair that are directly involved in the pathogenesis of epidemics of suicide and homicide, is far more effective in preventing or reversing those epidemics than investing our limited resources on treating or punishing people after they have been exposed to those risk factors. The US Public Health Service's Centers for Disease Control and Prevention have already established a Division of Violence Prevention. As two of their principal officers have written:[7]

---

[7] James A. Mercy and W. Rodney Hammond, "Preventing Homicide: A Public Health Perspective," pp. 274–94 in Smith and Zahn, eds., *Studying and Preventing Homicide*, p. 290.

The majority of existing violence prevention resources are spent trying to modify individual factors thought to contribute to violent behavior. Much less scientific and programmatic attention is given to addressing the social factors that may contribute to violence. . . . Yet scientific research suggests that marked social and economic disparities contribute to the etiology of violence in fundamental ways. . . . Poverty and the lack of real employment opportunities can promote violence by generating . . . low self-esteem, hopelessness about the future, and family instability. Racism and sexism exacerbate social and economic disparities. . . . More attention should be given to research and policy development that will guide us on how we might reduce violence through addressing larger social and economic issues.

One final implication of the data presented in this book is that they provide an empirical basis for evaluating different political parties and their social and economic policies and achievements – an assessment grounded in the human sciences, such as public health, preventive medicine, and economic and epidemiological statistics. These can serve as fact-based alternatives to the much more frequent opinion-based assertions and predictions concerning political parties, candidates, and policies. At a time when every knowledgeable person is calling for evidence-based medicine, isn't it time we also had evidence-based politics?

My point is that we will save more lives if we replace moral and political value judgments that are neither proveable nor unproveable with an empirically based set of findings that can be confirmed or disconfirmed. I offer this as a method for basing political thought and decision-making on factual knowledge concerning the social, political, economic, and psychological forces and processes that support, promote, and sustain human life, as opposed to those that lead to death, rather than basing political conclusions on assertions, opinions, or social and political ideologies as to what is fair or unfair, or what people "deserve" or do not "deserve."

One of the theoretical models and inspirations of this book, on many of whose insights the basic assumptions of this book are founded, was one of the greatest physicians of the nineteenth century, Rudolph Virchow (1821–1902).[8] He is perhaps most famous as the man who is credited with having made as many contributions as any one person in history to the project of transforming medicine from a crude set of practices based on tradition and superstition as often as on evidence – and which often did more harm than good – into the modern applied science that it has become, based on the empirical and theoretical foundations provided by both the natural and the human sciences. He is widely regarded as among the most important founders of the medical specialties of cellular pathology (it is largely due to him that everything from biopsies to autopsies are so central in modern medicine), public health, and preventive and social medicine (from improving housing and nutrition for the poor, to designing the first hygienic, pollution-free water supply and sewer system for Berlin), and as one of the pioneers of the social science called anthropology; and he made equally important contributions

[8] See L. Benaroyo, "Rudolf Virchow and the Scientific Approach to Medicine," *Endeavor*, 22: 114–17, 1998.

to the progressive politics of his time, an activity that he regarded as indissolubly one with functioning as a physician and healing diseases. In his "Report on the Typhus Outbreak of Upper Silesia" (1848), for example, he wrote that the outbreak could not be solved by treating individual patients with drugs or with minor changes in food, housing, or clothing laws, but only through radical action to promote the social and economic advancement of an entire population of (mostly) poor people. This conclusion is identical to what I am saying in this book about the epidemics of homicide and suicide from which the US periodically suffers. As a young man, Virchow fought in one of the revolutions of 1848, and later served for many years as one of Bismarck's main parliamentary adversaries in the Reichstag in Berlin. It was Virchow who proclaimed, in a series of bold and ringing statements, a set of conclusions that I will quote as the coda with which to conclude this book:

> The improvement of medicine will eventually prolong human life, but improvement of social conditions can achieve this result more rapidly and more successfully.[9] [That is why] physicians are the natural attorneys of the poor, and social problems fall to a large extent within their jurisdiction. As the science of man, medicine has

---

[9] Quoted in Howard Waitzkin, "One and a Half Centuries of Forgetting and Rediscovering: Virchow's Lasting Contributions to Social Medicine," *Social Medicine*, 1(1): 5–10, February 2006. Also quoted in Erwin H. Ackerknecht, *Rudolf Virchow: Doctor, Statesman, Anthropologist*, Madison: University of Wisconsin Press, 1953, p. 127, and in Leon Eisenberg, "Rudolph Ludwig Karl Virchow, Where Are You Now That We Need You?" *American Medicine* 159(19): 524–32, Sept. 1984, p. 527.

a duty to perform in recognizing these problems as its own and in offering the means by which a solution may be reached. Medical statistics will be our standard of measurement: we will weigh life for life and see where the dead lie thicker. . . . Medicine is a social science, and politics is simply medicine on a larger scale.[10]

---

[10] These were mottos of the weekly journal he founded, *Die Medizinische Reform (Medical Reform)*. The last sentence is in Rudolph Virchow, *Disease, Life, and Man* (trans. by L. J. Rather), Stanford: CA: Stanford University Press, 1958, p. 6, some of the essays from which also appeared in *Bulletin of the History of Medicine*, 30: 436–49, 537–43, 1956. These remarks are also quoted in George Rosen, "What Is Social Medicine? A Genetic Analysis of the Concept," *Bulletin of the History of Medicine*, 21: 674–733, 1947, p. 676, and in Eisenberg, "Rudolph Ludwig Karl Virchow," p. 525. See also D. Pridan, "Rudolf Virchow and Social Medicine in Historical Perspective," *Medical History*, 8: 274–84, 1964.

Appendix A

How Accurate and Complete Are the Data?

Although the US began publishing vital statistics data on a yearly basis in 1900, these data were not derived from all 48 of the then-existing states until 1933. The first report, in 1900, was based on only 10 states, mostly from New England. Additional states were added year after year, until by 1933 all 48 states were included. By 1912, the first year in which there was an electoral realignment from a Republican to a Democratic administration (when Woodrow Wilson replaced Taft), there were 22 states included; by 1920, the year of the next electoral realignment (from Wilson to the Republican Warren Harding), there were 34; and by 1932, when Roosevelt was elected, only 1 of the 48 states (Texas) was not included.

The fact that so many states were not included at first is not, however, as great a handicap to the research program I am presenting in this book as might at first appear, for several reasons. First, violent death rates have been reported separately for each of the three groups of states that constituted the death-registration area in 1900, 1910, and 1920, respectively, from the times when they were first included to 1933, when all states were included, and continuing on to 1940. When we examine those records, we find that all three groups of states showed the same pattern: net cumulative increases in violent death rates when Republicans were in power (1900–12 and 1921–32), and decreases when a Democrat was (1913–20). So it appears that the two parties were, so to speak, equal-opportunity employers – they increased or decreased violent death rates, no matter how many states were involved: whether it was a small sample, a larger one, or the whole country. In that sense, each "sample" of states was representative of the country as a whole, at least with respect to the larger question we are asking here: do violent death rates increase during Republican regimes and decrease during Democratic ones?

Second, if we examine only the data available from 1933 on, when all the states were being studied, we still have a huge database – 78 years' worth – and we again find the same result: massive increases in violent death rates under Republicans, and equally large decreases under Democrats. That is, we do not have to go back to 1900 in order to demonstrate this pattern, although that is no reason not to learn whatever we can from the data we do have prior to 1933.

A third alternative is to take advantage of the fact that the different states have been remarkably stable over time in the proportion to which they have contributed to the national violent death rates. For example, the Southern states have been known to have the highest homicide rates in the country, by far, whenever those rates were measured, ever since the first half of the nineteenth century, and they still do. The New England states, by contrast, have always had among the lowest homicide rates; the Western states, the highest suicide rates; and so on. And we know what the actual violent death rates were for each of the 48 states from 1933 on, and for an ever-increasing sample of the states from 1900 on. Finally, we know the size of the population for each state in any given year, and the age-distribution within each state.

Since we know that the murder rates in the New England states have always been lower than in the country as a whole, it is only reasonable to assume that a murder rate based on figures from the New England states alone, as in 1900, would almost certainly be lower than what the actual nation-wide murder rate was in that year. So the only question is: how do we correct for the missing data from the other states? By means of a sophisticated econometric statistical methodology that had proved successful in predicting future trends in various types of economic data, Eckberg[1] performed a rigorous "postdiction" of our national murder rates from 1900 through 1932 which has been accepted by most criminologists and epidemiologists as the "gold standard" for correcting for the missing homicide data for that era.[2]

---

[1] Eckberg, "Estimates of Early Twentieth-century U.S. Homicide Rates."

[2] Margaret A. Zahn and Patricia L. McCall have published a graph displaying Eckberg's corrected data for the period 1900–32, together with the data originally published by the US government's *Vital Statistics* reports, and comment that, although Eckberg's estimates of the pre-1933 homicide rates are higher than those enumerated in the original *Vital Statistics* reports, "the general trends are comparable. Both series display rates that fluctuate through time but show a general increase, peaking in 1906,

Since I do not know of any comparable recalculation of the reported suicide data, I devised a similar method of performing the same task for them (although we have every reason to believe that the reported suicide data during the early years of the century are not as discrepant from the true national rates as the homicide data were, since the discrepancy between the suicide rates in New England and the rest of the country is not nearly as great as it is for the homicide rates). We know what the ratio is between the complete national suicide rates, and those for each of the smaller samples of states (the 10 states whose rates were calculated in 1900, the 22 that were counted in 1912, and the 34 states that were registered in 1920), from 1933 on. Assuming that those samples of states contributed the same proportion to the total suicide rate throughout the times being studied (an assumption that is confirmed by all the data we do have), it is easy to calculate how much lower the actual national suicide rate is likely to have been from 1900 through 1932 than the reported rates indicated.

1921, and 1931" (Margaret A. Zahn and Patricia L. McCall, "Homicide in the 20th-Century United States: Trends and Patterns," pp. 10–30 in Smith and Zahn, eds., *Studying and Preventing Homicide*, p. 16, commenting on figure 2.1, p. 15). In other words, the shape of the two charts shows the same pattern, with lines that essentially parallel each other, but with Eckberg's data higher in both the peaks and the troughs, and with the difference gradually narrowing as more and more states were included in the government's data pool. For my purposes in this book, there is little relevant difference between the two charts, in that both show the same pattern: increases in the homicide rate during Republican administrations, and decreases during Democratic ones. I do believe, however, that Eckberg's data are very probably more accurate than those originally published, and I am happy to use them for purposes of calculating the differences attained under each political party.

Also, the suicide rates in the first ten (mostly New England) states (the 1900 sample) were higher than the national suicide rates, just as their homicide rates were lower than the true national rates. As a result, the uncorrected figures for total lethal violence rates (suicide plus homicide) are not as discrepant from what we can assume the true national rate would be as the suicide rates alone or the homicide rates alone would be. That is, the excess in the suicide rates and the under-estimate in the homicide rates partially cancel each other out, so that the total lethal violence rates are a closer approximation to the true rates than the suicide or homicide rates alone presumably are.

Since we have every reason to think that the corrected homicide and suicide data are more accurate than those reported by the government's own vital statisticians from 1900 through 1932 (and the revised figures are, after all, based on the more accurate data that we have from the time we had a complete sample of all 48 states from 1933 on), those are the figures that I refer to. Since the data that first caught my eye were the uncorrected data published in Holinger, I have included these data in figure B1 (which appears in appendix B). But since I was responsible for one of the data corrections (for suicide), let me immediately emphasize that Eckberg's and my corrected data both give results that are more favorable to the Republicans than the uncorrected government statistics are. That is, if I relied only on the uncorrected figures, the Republican record on lethal violence in America prior to 1933 would look even worse than it does with the corrected data. As a comparison between the uncorrected data (figure B1) and the corrected data (figure 1.1) shows, the figures that were originally published by the government's vital statistics branch before 1933 indicate that there were cumulative totals of 0.9 more suicides, 2.8 more homicides and 3.7 more total violent deaths per 100,000 per year during Republican administrations than the corrected data show; and that the discrepancy between the total violent death rates observed under the two parties was only 19.9 according to the corrected data, as compared with the uncorrected data, which would tell us (incorrectly) that the difference between the two parties was substantially greater, at 23.1. Thus, we would be unfair to the Republicans not to use corrected data for the period from 1900 through 1932. The results of their political actions were not as deadly as the original data would seem to indicate – although both sets of data are absolutely consistent with each other in showing that all three violent death rates (suicide, homicide, and the sum of suicide and homicide) increased during Republican administrations and decreased when Democrats were in power; and also in showing that there were significantly larger cumulative increases under Republicans, and larger cumulative decreases under Democrats, the longer the time-period being measured (what I have referred to as the "dose-response curve").

In order to be as fair and comprehensive as possible, I examined and compared all four groups of data:

- the uncorrected (originally reported) violent death rates, 1900–2007, which from 1900 through 1932 were based on an ever-enlarging but incomplete sample of states (figure B1),

- the violent death rates, 1900–2007, with the data for 1900–32 corrected to compensate for distortions created by the fact that not all states were yet included during those years in the national death registration area (figure 1.1),
- the death rates from the ever-increasing samples of states, as recorded from the presidential election year in which they were first included in the death-registration system (1900–40, 1912–40, 1920–40, and 1933–40), and
- the violent death rates for all 48 (and, later, 50) states from 1933 to 2007.

What I found was that all four of those groups of data come up with the same results: suicide and homicide rates both show net cumulative increases during Republican administrations, and net decreases during Democratic ones, and all of these differences are statistically significant. That remarkable fact in turn suggests that these correlations between party in power and death rate are in fact quite powerful and robust. No matter how you slice and dice the data in order to make sure you get the most accurate, comprehensive, and undistorted set of data possible, you keep getting the same results – net cumulative increases in rates of suicide, homicide, and the sum of the two during Republican administrations, and net decreases in all three measures during Democratic ones.

In order to clear up another possible misunderstanding, I should also reiterate that the death rates examined in this book are "age-adjusted." That is important since violence, like most other causes of death, is so strongly age-dependent, with higher murder rates (for both per-petrators and victims) among the young, and higher suicide rates among the elderly. As a result, changes in the proportion of the population that is of an age that is more or less vulnerable to a particular type of violence would create arbitrary changes in the resulting death rates that might appear to be related to some external event in the environment, such as a change in the ruling political party, but would in fact be merely an artifact of the "baby boom" or some other transient demographic variation. "Age-adjusting" is a way of holding the age-distribution of the population constant, for statistical purposes, so that that distortion will not happen. That is how we can be sure that the swings in violent death rates that are reported in these tables are not just reflections of swings in the percentage of people in the population of the nation as a whole who have reached a particular age.

Perhaps the principle involved will be most easily comprehended if one compares it to holding the value of the dollar constant in order to adjust for inflation, when one is comparing financial data for a series of different years, as when we speak, for example, of "1980 dollars." Clearly, for purposes of relative comparisons, it makes no difference whether one is using the year 1980, 1990, or 2000 as the basis for holding the purchasing power of the dollar constant; the important thing is merely to choose one year, and then stick with that one consistently.

The year I have chosen as the standard for age-adjusting is 1940. While that may seem rather remote from 2007, it is, I think, the best thing to do, for several reasons. First, it was the year that the National Center for Health Statistics recommended using until 1999, and it is the year on which all previous vital statistics had been based up to that point, going back to 1900. Second, it is closer in time to most of the years under study here than the year 2000. But third, and most important, it actually makes no difference to the questions I am asking in this book: that is, it is not going to distort the results of this investigation of the relationship between political parties and violent death rates throughout the twentieth century (and the beginning of the twenty-first). If death rates are increasing or decreasing under one party or the other, we will still be able to see the proportion by which those changes are occurring just as clearly using 1940 as the standard year for age-adjustment as we would if we used 2000. It is as easy to download the figures for the same years age-adjusted to 1970 or 2000 as to 1940, which I have also done, and it makes no difference to the question we are asking here: the three violent death rates all show a net cumulative increase under Republicans and a decrease under Democrats regardless of the year chosen as the standard for purposes of age-adjusting. So, while the particular year chosen is arbitrary and irrelevant, what would not work would be to use 1940 for part of the study and, say, 2000 for another part, so I have not done that when comparing changes in death rates from year to year.

Why have I not used the FBI's statistical publication, the *Uniform Crime Reports* (*UCR*), as the source for my homicide data? The answer is very simple: it is not nearly as complete or accurate as the vital statistics data compiled by the National Center for Health Statistics

(NCHS), since it relies on police reports and does not even receive data from all of the law-enforcement agencies in the country, and, furthermore, it does not provide age-adjusted data. The purpose of the *UCR* is mostly to provide such information as we have (incomplete though it is) about the perpetrators of various crimes (many of which are not reported to the police, if they were non-lethal, and many of the perpetrators of which are never apprehended), whereas I am asking questions about all known victims of lethal violence, all of whom are counted. Finally, the FBI's *UCR* is not even attempting to provide information about suicides, since those are no longer considered to be crimes, as they used to be in previous centuries.

The NCHS, by contrast, is counting victims, and thus it counts every death that is known to have occurred in this country, whether violent or non-violent, and has data available to it from every coroner, inquest, autopsy, and death certificate pronouncing the cause of death. While it is not perfect, as nothing human ever is, it is incomparably more trustworthy, comprehensive, and accurate than the *UCR* is about death rates, and is the only source of data that is sufficiently accurate to be useful for scientific purposes, in my opinion. If you merely want information about perpetrators, however, the *UCR* is the most extensive source of data we have, incomplete though it is, and that is the purpose it should be used for.

Appendix B

Figures and tables

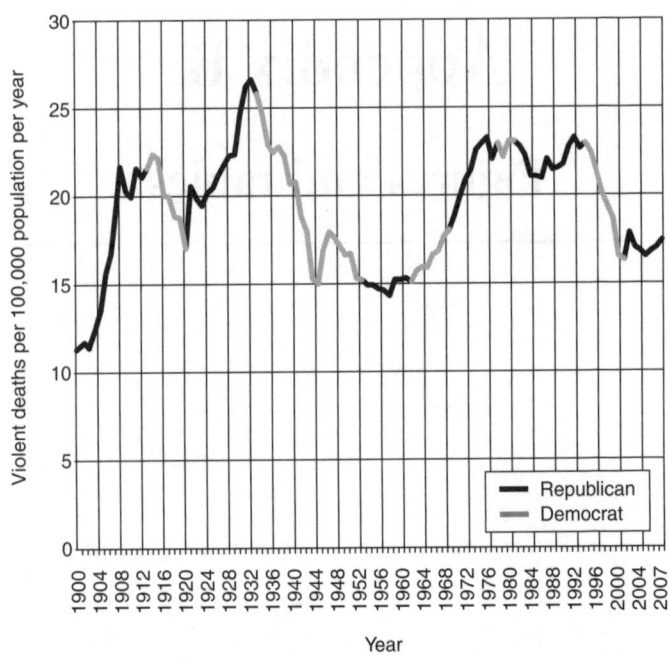

Figure B1   1900–2007 Violent Death Rates Age-Adjusted to
Standard Year 1940 with Data from 1900–1932. Not Corrected to
Adjust for the Non-Inclusion of Some States Prior to 1933

Source: Holinger, *Violent Deaths in the United States*

Table B1: Rates of unemployment under Democratic vs. Republican presidents, United States, 1900–2008

Party	President	Years	Unemployment rate, beginning of term	Unemployment rate, end of term	Increase/ decrease
Republican	McKinley, T. Roosevelt, Taft	1900–12	5.0	5.9	+0.9
Democratic	Wilson	1913–20	5.9	5.2	−0.7
Republican	Harding, Coolidge, Hoover	1921–32	5.2	22.9	+17.7
Democratic	F. D. Roosevelt, Truman	1933–52	22.9	3.0	−19.9
Republican	Eisenhower	1953–60	3.0	5.5	+2.5
Democratic	J. F. Kennedy, L. B. Johnson	1961–8	5.5	3.6	−1.9
Republican	Nixon, Ford	1969–76	3.6	7.7	+4.1
Democratic	Carter	1977–80	7.7	7.2	−0.5
Republican	Reagan, Bush	1981–92	7.2	7.5	+0.3
Democratic	Clinton	1993–2000	7.5	4.0	−3.5
Republican	Bush Jr.	2001–8	4.0	5.8	+1.8

Net change: Republicans: +27.3%; Democrats: −26.5%.
Net cumulative difference between the two parties: 53.8%.
Source: Bureau of Labor Statistics, US Department of Labor.

Table B2: Duration of unemployment under Democratic vs. Republican presidents, Post-war United States, 1948–2003

Party	President	Years	Average weeks unemployed, beginning of term	Average weeks unemployed, end of term	Increase/ decrease
Democratic	Truman	1948–52	8.6	8.4	−0.2
Republican	Eisenhower	1953–60	8.4	12.8	+4.4
Democratic	J. F. Kennedy, L. B. Johnson	1961–8	12.8	8.4	−4.4
Republican	Nixon, Ford	1969–76	8.4	15.8	+7.4
Democratic	Carter	1977–80	15.8	11.9	−3.9
Republican	Reagan, Bush	1981–92	11.9	17.7	+5.8
Democratic	Clinton	1993–2000	17.7	12.6	−5.1
Republican	Bush Jr.	2000–3	12.6	19.6	+7.0

Net Change: Republicans: +24.6 *weeks*; Democrats: −13.6 *weeks*.
Net cumulative difference between the two parties: 38.2 *weeks (9 months.)*
Source: Bureau of Labor Statistics, US Department of Labor.

Appendices

Table B3: Red States vs. Blue States

Violent death rate differences according to state voting patterns, Democratic vs. Republican, 2000 and 2004

2000	Red States ($n = 30$)		Blue States ($n = 20$)		Significance	
Death rate						
(per 100,000)	Mean	SD	Mean	SD	T	p
Homicide	5.70	2.85	4.23	2.43	1.90	0.064
Suicide	13.0	2.89	10.0	2.95	3.57	0.001*
Total	18.7	3.80	14.2	4.02	4.01	0.000*
2004	Red States ($n = 31$)		Blue States ($n = 19$)		Significance	
Death rate						
(per 100,000)	Mean	SD	Mean	SD	T	p
Homicide	5.70	2.67	4.01	2.15	2.38	0.021*
Suicide	13.9	3.19	10.2	2.70	4.28	0.000*
Total	19.6	4.04	14.2	2.90	5.16	0.000*

* = significant

Source: National Center for Health Statistics, Centers for Disease Control and Prevention, U.S. Public Health Service. Retrieved from: "CDC – Injury – WISQARS (Web-Based Injury Query and Reporting System)"

Bibliography

Adorno, Theodor W., E. Frenkel-Brunswick, D. J. Levinson, and R. N. Sanford, *The Authoritarian Personality*, New York: Harper and Row, 1950

Alexander, Michelle, *The New Jim Crow: Mass Incarceration in the Age of Colorblindness*, New York and London: The New Press, 2010

Altemeyer, Robert, *Enemies of Freedom: Understanding Right-Wing Authoritarianism*, San Francisco: Jossey-Bass, 1988

Altemeyer, Robert, *Right-Wing Authoritarianism*, Winnipeg: University of Manitoba Press, 1981

Altemeyer, Robert, *The Authoritarian Specter*, Cambridge, MA, and London: Harvard University Press, 1996

Ayers, Edward L., *Vengeance and Justice: Crime and Punishment in the 19th-Century American South*, New York and Oxford: Oxford University Press, 1984

Bartels, Larry M., *Unequal Democracy: The Political Economy of the New Gilded Age*, New York: Russell Sage Foundation, 2007

Benaroyo, L., "Rudolf Virchow and the Scientific Approach to Medicine," *Endeavor*, 22: 114–17, 1998

Bernstein, Jared, Lawrence Mishel, and Chauna Brocht, "Any Way You Cut It: Income Inequality on the Rise Regardless of How It's Measured," Briefing Paper, Economic Policy Institute, n.d. Downloaded from http://epinet.org

Blumenthal, Sidney, "Crime Pays," *The New Yorker*, May 9, 1994, p. 44

Chiricos, Theodore G., "Rates of Crime and Unemployment: An Analysis of Aggregate Research Evidence," *Social Problems*, 34(2): 187–212, April 1987

Cook, Philip J., and Mark H. Moore, "Guns, Gun Control, and Homicide," pp. 246–73 in M. Dwayne Smith and Margaret A. Zahn, eds., *Studying and Preventing Homicide: Issues and Challenges*, Thousand Oaks, CA, London, and New Delhi: SAGE Publications, 1999

Cottle, Thomas, *Hardest Times: The Trauma of Long-Term Unemployment*, Amherst: University of Massachusetts Press, 2001

Eaton, Joseph W., and Robert J. Weil, *Culture and Mental Disorders*, Glencoe, IL: The Free Press, 1955

Eckberg, D. L., "Estimates of Early Twentieth-century U.S. Homicide Rates: An Econometric Forecasting Approach," *Demography* 32: 1–16, 1995

Emerson, Ralph Waldo, *Journals*, ed. E. W. Emerson and W. E. Forbes, Boston, 1909–14, Vol. IV

Ford, Henry Jones, *The Rise and Growth of American Politics*, New York: Macmillan, 1898

Galbraith, James K., *Created Unequal: The Crisis in American Pay*, New York: The Free Press, 1998

Gilligan, James, *Preventing Violence*, London and New York: Thames and Hudson, 2001

Gilligan, James, "Shame, Guilt and Violence," *Social Research* 70 (4): 1149–80, 2003

Gilligan, James, "Spare the Rod: Why Are More American Children Victims and Perpetrators of Violence than Those of Any Other Developed Country?" in James Garbarino, ed., *A Child's Right to a Healthy Environment*, New York: Springer, in press, 2010

Gilligan, James, "The Last Mental Hospital," *Psychiatric Quarterly* 72(1): 45–61, 2001

Gilligan, James, *Violence: Our Deadly Epidemic and Its Causes*, New York: Grosset/Putnam, 1996 (also published in paperback as *Violence: Reflections on a National Epidemic*, New York: Vintage Books, 1997)

Gilligan, James, and Bandy Lee, "Beyond the Prison Paradigm: From Provoking Violence to Preventing It by Creating 'Anti-Prisons' (Residential Colleges and Therapeutic Communities)," in John Devine, James Gilligan, Klaus A. Miczek, Rashid Shaikh, and Donald Pfaff, eds., *Youth Violence: Scientific Approaches to Prevention*, *Annals of the New York Academy of Sciences*, 1036: 300–24, 2004

Gilligan, James, and Bandy Lee, "The Resolve to Stop the Violence Project: Reducing Violence in the Community through a Jail-Based Initiative," *Journal of Public Health*, 27(2): 143–8, June 2005

Gilmore, David D., ed., *Honor and Shame and the Unity of the Mediterranean*, Washington, DC: American Anthropological Association, 1987

Greenberg, Kenneth S., *Honor and Slavery*, Princeton: Princeton University Press, 1996

Hetherington, Marc J., and Jonathan D. Weiler, *Authoritarianism and Polarization in American Politics*, Cambridge: Cambridge University Press, 2009

Hojman, Daniel, and Felipe Kast, "On the Measurement of Income Dynamics," Harvard University, Kennedy School Working Paper, Oct. 2009

Holinger, Paul C., *Violent Deaths in the United States*, New York: Guilford Press, 1987

Hostetler, John A., *Hutterite Life*, Scottdale, PA: Herald Press, 1983

Hostetler, John A., *Hutterite Society*, Baltimore, MD: Johns Hopkins University Press, 1974

Hostetler, John A., and Gertrude Enders Huntington, *The Hutterites in North America*, Fort Worth: Harcourt Brace, 1996

Hsieh, Ching-Chi, and M. D. Pugh, "Poverty, Income Inequality, and Violent Crime: A Meta-Analysis of Recent Aggregate Data Studies," *Criminal Justice Review*, 18: 182–202, 1993; reprinted as pp. 278–96 in Ichiro Kawachi, Bruce P. Kennedy, and Richard G. Wilkinson, eds., *The Society and Population Health Reader*, Vol. I: *Income Inequality and Health*, New York: The New Press, 1999

Juergensmeyer, Mark, *Terror in the Mind of God: The Global Rise of Religious Violence*, 3rd edn. (Comparative Studies in Religion and Society, 13), Berkeley: University of California Press, 2003

Kaplan, Bert, and Thomas F. Plaut, *Personality in a Communal Society: An Analysis of the Mental Health of the Hutterites*, Lawrence, KS: University of Kansas Press, 1956

Kaplan, Justin, gen. ed., *Bartlett's Familiar Quotations*, Boston: Little, Brown, 1992

Karmen, Andrew, *New York Murder Mystery: The True Story behind the Crime Crash of the 1990s*, New York: New York University Press, 2000

Kauffman, Kelsey, *Prison Officers and Their World*, Cambridge, MA: Harvard University Press, 1988

Krug, Etienne G., Linda L. Dahlberg, James A. Mercy, Anthony B. Zwi, and Rafael Lozano, *World Report on Violence and Health*, Geneva: World Health Organization, 2002

LaFree, Gary, and K. A. Drass, "The Effect of Changes in Intraracial Income Inequality and Educational Attainment on Changes in Arrest Rates for African Americans and Whites, 1957 to 1990," *American Sociological Review*, 61: 614–34, 1996

Land, Kenneth C., Patricia L. McCall, and Lawrence E. Cohen, "Structural Covariates of Homicide Rates: Are There Any Invariances across Time and Social Space?" *The American Journal of Sociology*, 95(4): 922–63, Jan., 1990

Lee, Bandy, and James Gilligan, "The Resolve to Stop the Violence Project: Transforming an In-House Culture of Violence through a Jail-Based Programme," *Journal of Public Health*, 27(2): 149–55, June 2005

Lukas, J. Anthony, *Common Ground: A Turbulent Decade in the Lives of Three American Families*, New York: Knopf, 1985

Major, L., customer review of Thomas J. Cottle, *Hardest Times: The Trauma of Long-Term Unemployment*. Downloaded from Amazon.com: Books

Mercy, James A., and W. Rodney Hammond, "Preventing Homicide: A Public Health Perspective," pp. 274–94 in M. Dwayne Smith and Margaret A. Zahn, eds., *Studying and Preventing Homicide: Issues and Challenges*, Thousand Oaks, CA, London, and New Delhi: SAGE Publications, 1999

Messner, Steven F., and Richard Rosenfeld, "Social Structure and Homicide," pp. 27–41 in M. Dwayne Smith and Margaret A. Zahn, eds., *Homicide: A Sourcebook of Social Research*, Thousand Oaks, CA, London, and New Delhi: SAGE Publications, 1999

Michaels, David, *Doubt Is Their Product: How Industry's Assault on Science Threatens Your Health*, Oxford and New York: Oxford University Press, 2008.

Miller, Michael, "A Suicide Map of the U.S.," *Boston Globe*, August 22, 2004

Miranda, P., *Communism in the Bible*, Maryknoll, NY: Orbis Books, 1982

Neustadt, Richard E., *Presidential Power and the Modern Presidents: The Politics of Leadership from Roosevelt to Reagan*, New York: The Free Press, 1990

Newman, Katherine, *No Shame in My Game: The Working Poor in the Inner City*, New York: Vintage Books and Russell Sage Foundation, 1999

Nietzsche, Friedrich, "Beyond Good and Evil" and "The Genealogy of Morals," in *Basic Writings of Nietzsche*, trans., ed., and with an Introduction and notes by Walter Kaufmann, New York: Random House, 2000

Nisbett, Richard E., and Dov Cohen, *Culture of Honor: The Psychology of Violence in the South*, Boulder, CO, and Oxford: Westview Press, 1996

Page, A., S. Morrell, and R. Taylor, "Suicide and Political Regime in New South Wales and Australia during the 20th Century," *Journal of Epidemiological Community Health*, 6: 766–72, 2002

Patterson, Orlando, *Rituals of Blood: Consequences of Slavery in Two American Centuries*, New York: Basic Books, 1998

Patterson, Orlando, *Slavery and Social Death: A Comparative Study*, Cambridge, MA: Harvard University Press, 1982

Peristiany, J. G., *Honour and Shame: The Values of Mediterranean Society*, Chicago: University of Chicago Press, 1966

Peristiany, J. G., and Julian Pitt-Rivers, eds., "Introduction," in *Honor and Grace in Anthropology*, Cambridge: Cambridge University Press, 1992

Perkinson, Robert, *Texas Tough: The Rise of America's Prison Empire*, New York: Metropolitan Books, Henry Holt and Company, 2010

Pew Research Center for the People and the Press, "The 2005 Political Typology: Beyond Red vs. Blue: Republicans Divided about Role of Government – Democrats by Social and Personal Values," May 10, 2005. Downloaded from www.people-press.org

Pitt-Rivers, Julian, "Honor," pp. 503–11 in *International Encyclopedia of the Social Sciences*, 1968

Pitt-Rivers, Julian, "Honor and Social Status," pp. 19–77 in J. G. Peristiany, ed., *Honour and Shame: The Values of Mediterranean Society*, Chicago: University of Chicago Press, 1966

Ponnuru, Ramesh, *The Party of Death: The Democrats, the Media, the Courts, and the Disregard for Human Life*, 2006

Popper, Karl, *The Logic of Scientific Discovery*, London: Hutchinson, 1959

Reiss, Albert J. Jr., and Jeffrey A. Roth, eds. (Panel on the Understanding and Control of Violent Behavior, National Research Council, National Academy of Sciences), *Understanding and Preventing Violence*, Vol. I, Washington, DC: National Academy Press, 1993

Rochlin, Gregory, *Man's Aggression: The Defense of the Self*, Boston: Gambit, 1973

Rosaldo, Michelle, ed., *Towards an Anthropology of the Emotions: Rethinking Shame and Guilt* (Proceedings of a Symposium of the American Anthropological Association), Washington, DC: American Anthropological Association, 1983

Sabini, John, "Aggression in the Laboratory," pp. 343–371 in Irwin L. Kutash, Samuel B. Kutash, and Louis B. Schlesinger, eds., *Violence: Perspectives on Murder and Aggression*, San Francisco: Jossey-Bass, 1978

Schlesinger, Arthur Jr., *The Imperial Presidency*, Boston: Houghton Mifflin, 1989

Schwartz, Sunny (with David Boodell), *Dreams from the Monster Factory: A Tale of Prison, Redemption and One Woman's Fight to Restore Justice to All* (with an Introduction by James Gilligan), New York: Scribner, 2009

Shaw, M., D. Dorling, and G. Davey Smith, "Mortality and Political Climate: How Suicide Rates Have Risen during Periods of Conservative Government, 1901–2000," *Journal of Epidemiological Community Health*, 56: 723–5, 2002

Silberman, Charles E., *Criminal Violence, Criminal Justice*, New York: Random House, 1978

Thomas, Herbert E., "Experiencing a Shame Response as a Precursor to Violence," *Bulletin of the American Academy of Psychiatry Law*, 23(4): 587–93

Tomkins, Silvan S., "Ideology and Affect," pp. 109–67 in E. Virginia Demos, ed., *Exploring Affect: The Selected Writings of Silvan S. Tomkins* (Studies in Emotion and Social Interaction), Cambridge: Cambridge University Press, 1995

Tomkins, Silvan S., "The Right and the Left: A Basic Dimension of Ideology and Personality," pp. 389–411 in R. W. White, ed., *The Study of Lives*, New York: Atherton Press, 1963

West, Donald J., *Murder Followed by Suicide*. Cambridge, MA: Harvard University Press, 1967

Wilkinson, Richard, "Why is Violence More Common Where Inequality Is Greater?" pp. 1–12 in John Devine, James Gilligan, Klaus A. Miczek, Rashid Shaikh, and Donald Pfaff, eds., *Youth Violence: Scientific Approaches to Prevention, Annals of the New York Academy of Sciences*, 1036, 2004

Wilkinson, Richard, and Kate Pickett, *The Spirit Level: Why Greater Equality Makes Societies Stronger*, New York: Bloomsbury Press, 2009

Wilson, William Julius, *When Work Disappears: The World of the New Urban Poor*, New York: Vintage, 1996

Wolcott, James, "Red State Babylon," *Vanity Fair*, Nov. 2006, p. 162

Wolff, Edward N., *Top Heavy: The Increasing Inequality of Wealth in America and What Can Be Done about It* (An Expanded Edition of a Twentieth Century Fund Report), New York: The New Press, 1996

Wolfgang, Marvin E., and Franco Ferracuti, *The Sub-Culture of Violence*, Beverly Hills, CA: Sage Publications, 1982

Wolfgang, Marvin E., *Patterns in Criminal Homicide*, New York: Science Editions, John Wiley & Sons, 1966 (original publication: Philadelphia, PA: University of Pennsylvania Press, 1958)

Wyatt-Brown, Bertram, *Southern Honor: Ethics and Behavior in the Old South*, Oxford and New York: Oxford University Press, 1982; abridged version: *Honor and Violence in the Old South*, Oxford and New York: Oxford University Press, 1986

Zahn, Margaret A., and Patricia L. McCall, "Homicide in the 20th-Century United States: Trends and Patterns," pp. 10–30 in M. Dwayne Smith and Margaret A. Zahn, eds., *Studying and Preventing Homicide: Issues and Challenges*, Thousand Oaks, CA, London, and New Delhi: SAGE Publications, 1999

Index

Index

Index

Index

Index

Index

recidivism 151
  preventing of through college
    education in prisons 90–1,
    153
Red State / Blue State
  differences 164, 186
  attitudes and values of
    different population groups
    125–6
  and capital punishment
    130–1, 134
  cultural 132–9
  graph *209*
  gun ownership 131, 138
  imprisonment rate 131–2
  lethal violence rates
    compared 123–4, 125,
    129–30, *209*
  and suicide 129
Red States 10, 93, 123–54
  composition 132
  and honor and shame culture
    133–4
  see also Southern states
redundancy *see* unemployment
Republican Party /
  Republicanism
  and authoritarianism 143
  benefits of high crime 82–4
  claims to be party of
    prosperity and public safety
    69
  dismantling of college
    education in prisons 92
  "divide and conquer"
    strategy 75–8, 80, 82, 84,
    94, 182
  and economic growth 61
  economic policies 64
  and GDP 52
  and GNP 62, 64

  and gun ownership 93, 127
  and income/economic
    inequality 52, 63, 73, 167
  increase in lethal violence
    rates 3–4, 7, 8, *12*, 13, 14,
    17–18, 19, 20–2, 23, 24,
    25, 26–31, 34–5, 36, 38,
    48, 69, 156–8, 161, 163,
    168, 169, 196, 201
  and poverty 69, 75, 84,
    160
  and racial inequality 76–7,
    167–8
  reasons for electoral success
    72–86, 94
  and recessions 48, 54, 56–61,
    64
  reduction of liberty and
    defeating pursuit of
    happiness 168–9
  and shame 141
  Southern strategy 21–2, 75–7,
    137, 167, 188
  and unemployment 52, 53,
    54–6, 65, 67, 159, 165,
    186
  and wealth concentration
    72–3, 74–5, 79
  and wealth inequality 52
  see also Red State / Blue State
    differences
Republican voters 10, 141
  views on force and violence
    compared with Democrat
    voters 126–9
right-wing politics 105
  and authoritarianism 139,
    142
  and shame 104, 109
risk factors vs. protective
  factors 26–35

Index

Index